INSIGHT COMPACT GUIDE

YORK

Compact Guide: York is the ideal quick-reference guide to this ancient city and its surroundings. It tells you everything you need to know about York's attractions, from its magnificent Minster to its medieval walls, from narrow streets lined with half-timbered houses to fascinating museums focusing on Romans, Vikings, army history and steam trains.

This is one of 133 Compact Guides produced by the editors of Insight Guides, whose books have set the standard for visual travel guides since 1970. Packed with information, arranged in easy-to-follow routes, and lavishly illustrated with photographs, this book not only steers you round York but also gives you fascinating insights into local life.

APA PUBLICATIONS
Part of the Langenscheidt Publishing Group

Star Attractions

An instant reference to some of York's most popular tourist attractions to help you on your way.

York Minster p16

The Shambles p30

Jorvik Viking Centre p31

National Railway Museum p40

Castle Museum p33

Museum Gardens p41

Bar Walls p21, 35, 50 & 53

Stonegate p23

Clifford's Tower p 32

Castle Howard p 57

Merchant Adventurers' Hall p51

Introduction

Places

Culture

Leisure

Practical Information

York – City of All Ages

Opposite: pinnacle of Gothic art

The Shambles

York is a city that encompasses all of England's history. Encircled by medieval walls and gateways that still bear the scars of battle, its great Gothic cathedral lies surrounded by quaint narrow streets. The bustling life of the golden Elizabethan age can be imagined in the half-timbered houses of the Shambles and the elegance of Georgian England savoured in the pizzeria that now inhabits the old Assembly Rooms. The power and authority of ancient Rome can be glimpsed in the remains of legionary fortress walls, and the all-conquering Vikings have left the wooden walls of their Jorvik settlement in Coppergate.

York has seen invaders come and go, battles raging around its walls and kings and queens demanding entry at its gates. 'The history of York is the history of England,' declared George VI. And each age and each great event has contrived to leave behind some legacy of its passing. The result is a modern city that is able to illustrate its own intriguing story through its streets, its buildings and its stained glass. It has become a mixture of all former ages with some 21st-century additions thrown in to add spice, and controversy. And despite all the temptations created by the tourist trade, it remains a living, working, shopping city that resolutely refuses to turn itself into a museum.

5

Location and size

The city of 181,000 inhabitants bestrides the River Ouse and dominates the Plain of York. It stands at the halfway point between London, the capital of England, and Edinburgh, the capital of Scotland. Often in its history York has itself assumed the role of capital of the North and still remains a centre for administration, trade, and the law – a garrison town and a cathedral city.

One of many fine watering holes

Since early times it has been the home of the Archbishop of York, the Primate of England, who is second only to the Archbishop of Canterbury in the hierarchy of the Anglican Church. When Yorkshire was one county, York was the county town – ideally placed where the three ridings or administrative areas converged. Since 1963 it has also been a university city with a growing reputation as a centre of academic excellence. The university at Heslington has influenced the cultural and economic life of the city by creating the beginnings of a Silicon Valley on its Science Park.

For the success of its geographical location the city can thank the Romans, who picked the spot with their usual practicality. The Ouse provided them with access to the sea and the confluence with the River Foss gave their fortress water protection on two sides. When the legions marched away, Anglo-Saxon and

then Viking invaders saw the strategic convenience of the site and moved in to settle. Centuries later, York was on the coach route between London and Scotland and later still George Hudson, the city's Railway King, made certain that the main line north passed through his city – as it still does today.

George Hudson 'off the rails'

Economy

York's road and river links quickly established it as a trading centre. Even in Roman times ships with wine from Bordeaux were docking at its quays. Medieval merchants set up a powerful Merchant Adventurers trading company. Specialist markets dealing in butter, meat, animals and hay so crowded the streets that houses, even church graveyards, were demolished to give the traders more room. For miles around, York was the place to go to sell and buy.

But even though the railways came early to York the city slowly lost out economically to the more vigorously commercial and industrial towns of the West Riding. After a period of stagnation York came to rely on a mixture of railways and chocolate for its prosperity. Two famous confectionery firms, Rowntree and Terry's, were the main sources of employment, along with the building of railway coaches at the headquarters of the London and North Eastern Railway Company. For a time, York slipped into a backwater and assumed a genteel, aloof shabbiness before making a post-war revival.

Life is quiet along the Ouse

Tourism

The re-awakening started in 1951 with the Festival of Britain when York was chosen as one of the provincial centres for the celebrations. The city's medieval Mystery Plays were revived after a gap of 400 years and their success gave York its first taste of tourism. A series of events, not all of them welcome, thrust the city on to the national and international stage. In 1961 the Duke of Kent married Miss Katherine Worsley in the cathedral romantically decorated with white roses, the symbol of the Royal House of York. The event was attended by the Queen and 62 members of the Royal family and watched by millions on television. The Minster itself then unwillingly added to the city's publicity with the discovery in 1968 that the Central Tower was in danger of collapse and that £2 million was needed for repairs. And in 1971 the Queen was back with the Household Cavalry riding through the streets as part of the city's 1,900th birthday party

Mystery Plays in the Museum Gardens

Still more royalty, including most of the crowned heads of Scandinavia, paid visits when archaeologists found the remains of Viking York during excavations in Coppergate in 1976. And, as if the city had not been given enough media exposure to boost its tourist trade, lightning struck out of a summer night sky in 1984 and destroyed the cathe-

Artisans are still at work

dral's south transept. Graphic images of the leaping flames were beamed around the world.

Yet York did not embrace its tourism bonanza wholeheartedly. A slightly insular population resented the overcrowded car parks and cafés and 'other people' trampling over 'our city'. Some even took to wearing a badge: 'I'm not a tourist, I live here!' But the resentment died as the economic benefits became all too obvious. Today around 4 million visitors pour millions of pounds a year into the local economy, and in the wake of the tourists have come high-quality shops and more restaurants, facilities and entertainments – far more than the local population could expect to support by itself. York has embraced tourism and taken on a more cosmopolitan attitude to life as a result. Sightseeing buses circle the city and every sort of visitor 'experience' is on offer from Roman and Viking to Medieval and Georgian. Voluntary guides take visitors on explorations into every nook and cranny of the old city. Even the city's ghosts – and there seem to be scores of them – have been prodded out of their hiding places for the benefit of the tourist trade. Ghostly tale tellers vie with each other to give visitors a shivering walk through the backstreets, helped by strategically placed colleagues in dark corners. The insularity of the locals has faded.

Viking Jorvik

7

Preservation and conservation

Over the years organisations and individuals have fought hard to preserve the city. In the early 19th century the city fathers wanted to pull down the Bar Walls and sell off the stone because they were short of cash for restoring one of the bridges. There was pressure for the removal of ancient gateways which were designed to keep invaders out but were obstacles to bringing traders in. Protest groups saved the gateways but did not succeed in keeping all the barbicans. Only one survives, at Walmgate *(see page 53)*. And

The White Rose

Heritage preserved at Lady Pickett's Yard

Stonegate

Georgian detail

when a new road and street was needed at St Leonard's, down came a stretch of the defence wall of St Mary's Abbey.

York was fortunate not to be badly scarred by the reconstruction work which struck some historic towns after World War II. There was an outcry when a row of old houses was demolished in Goodramgate to be replaced with starkly modern shop facades behind pillarless concrete arches. The York Civic Trust led a battle to protect the city's old buildings from demolition and proposed instead careful renovation and adaption to new uses. Their plea was to preserve the city's uniqueness rather than create shopping streets that were a replica of every other shopping street in the country. Such was the concern that historic cities could be destroyed by commercial pressures that in 1968 York was chosen for a special study by the town planner Viscount Esher. Not all his ideas were adopted but gradually city centre traffic was controlled, then excluded, and all redevelopment in the historic core strictly regulated. His suggestion for new town housing in the semi-derelict area of Aldwark *(see page 50)* was adopted and has successfully brought people back to live in the city centre, reversing a century of flight to the suburbs.

Various conservation societies have refurbished old property and, to keep the city on its toes, the Civic Trust in particular became an arbiter of good taste, producing an annual list of 'bouquets and brickbats': praising a piece of good design here and criticising the 'wrong colour' on a Georgian door there. Frustrated architects protested that a bland Neo-Georgian style was being imposed on everything new and that good, modern design could blend with the old. In a city which has showcase architecture of all ages, they had a point – but where modernity was permitted, such as in Stonebow and Davygate, not everyone is convinced that it has been successful.

Archaeology

Knock down any building in central York and you will find another underneath it and probably still more below – each one presenting a perfect opportunity for finding out more about the city's past. Developers inevitably found archaeologists at their elbow pleading for more time to explore but the York Archaeological Trust proved that 'rescue archaeology' could be done without confrontation.

With the help of both national legislation and local arrangements the archaeologists were given time to dig ahead of building work and it became a two-way benefit. The Trust's growing knowledge of what was likely to be found underground often allowed developers to avoid expensive foundation problems. And when Viking York was discovered under Coppergate, the Trust showed that archaeology, far from holding up development, could lead to profitable commercial ventures. The Jorvik Viking Centre created by the Trust on the site of the dig has not only paid for itself but has become an asset which contributes to the cost of archaeology in the city.

Until the post-war period, archaeology in the city had been dominated by the Roman presence. Street patterns largely followed the Roman layout. The well documented symmetry of Roman fortresses made Roman remains relatively easy to find even though they were usually some 10 ft (3 m) under modern street levels. Where sites have been cleared for rebuilding, Roman walls, towers and barrack blocks have popped up in all the expected places. A public house in St Sampson's Square has a glass panel in the floor so visitors can look down into a Roman bathhouse. But what was unexpected was the discovery of a Roman sewer under Church Street which the archaeologists explored like cavers and fitted out with electric lights. And underneath York Minster the collapsed drums of a column which stood in the arcaded Roman forum of Eboracum were found by workmen giving the Central Tower new concrete 'feet'.

The Multangular Tower

Thanks to the Archaeological Trust a great deal of light has been shed on the Dark Ages in York – the years after the Romans marched away and before the Normans produced their Domesday records. Modern techniques have allowed archaeologists to sift and interpret occupation layers which Roman levels above 19th-century historical explorers largely ignored. Information has been gathered from seeds, pollen, fragments of bone, pieces of wood and even snail shells. The eating habits and life style of Viking York have been revealed through the richness of its floor 'droppings'.

9

St Mary's Abbey ruins

Similarly, life in Anglo-Saxon York became clearer after the archaeologists explored a site ahead of the building of a new hotel in Fishergate. This turned out to be the long lost Anglo-Saxon Eoforwic. Finds of continental pottery suggested that the Anglo Saxons, too, used York as a trading town.

Present and future

The flurry of redevelopments and of 'rescue archaeology' has subsided, giving the historians time to catch up with their writing and research. New office blocks have appeared on the skyline – all obeying a local rule not to overtop the cathedral. Although railway coach building has declined in the city and jobs making chocolate have been transplanted to the continent, the City Council has been successful in attracting government departments as they become 'decentralised' from London and Yorkshire has taken Kent's traditional crown as the Garden of England for its natural beauty and as a preserve of traditional English life.

Inside the Theatre Royal

Historical Highlights

AD71 Roman Governor, Petilius Cerialis, builds first earth rampart and stake fortress at the confluence of the Rivers Foss and Ouse. He establishes the IX Legion in what becomes Eboracum.

117 Emperor Hadrian, in Britain building Hadrian's Wall to protect England from the 'barbarians' further north, uses York as a base.

208 Emperor Severus sets up Imperial Court in York. The city becomes capital of Lower Britain, and for a time administrative centre for the Roman World.

306 Constantine made emperor of the Roman Empire in York after his father Emperor Constantius died in the city.

410 Legions abandon York. Emperor Honorius tells the civilian population in Britain, including York, to look after its own defence.

524 Anglian settlers move into the area from the continent and eventually drive the British out of York. The city becomes Eoforwic.

627 First wooden church, dedicated to St Paul, built on the site of the Minster. Anglo-Saxon King Edwin accepts Christianity and is baptised in the church by Paulinus. Edwin is killed six years later in battle and the church destroyed.

685 St Cuthbert consecrated bishop in new rebuilt stone Minster. In 741 this Minster is burned during fighting between warring factions in the north; a new Minster built in stone in 780.

866 Viking raids along the coast eventually become invasions with the Vikings slowly taking over the north of England. Vikings capture York in 868 and establish control over the area.

954 Viking Eric Bloodaxe expelled from York by Anglo-Saxon King Edgar.

1000 A monk's account of the life of St Oswald records the population of York as 30,000.

1066 Viking army sails up River Ouse. King Harold defeats them at Stamford Bridge near York as William of Normandy lands at Hastings.

1068 William conquers England and builds a castle at York to subdue the northern English and Danish armies. It is destroyed within a year but then rebuilt. The Minster is burned during the fighting, but the Normans build a new one.

1086 The population of York drops to 5,000.

1190 Anti-semitic riots. Jews living in York take refuge in Clifford's Tower where some 150 die by their own hand or at the hands of the mob when the tower is set on fire.

1291 Work starts on a new, larger Minster.

1300–1400 Powerful guilds become established and control the city's trade and commerce. The population rises to 10,000.

1328 Edward III marries Philippa of Hainault in the Minster; the marriage is attended by virtually every member of the English aristocracy.

1455–85 Wars of the Roses between the House of York (the white rose) and the House of Lancaster (red rose).

1472 The Minster completed. It is the largest Gothic cathedral north of the Alps.

1530 Horse racing begins at Clifton. Plague reduces population to 8,000.

1572 Medieval Mystery Plays banned after clergy complain of unseemly disorders.

1604 Guy Fawkes of York is arrested trying to blow up Parliament. Plague causes 3,512 deaths.

1606 River Ouse freezes over and games are played on ice including a horse race from Marygate to Skeldergate.

1631 Plague returns to York. City gates closed and breaches in the walls sealed to prevent the pestilence spreading. Population 12,000.

1639 Charles I sets up Royal Mint in York and a printing press in St William's College to circulate Royal leaflet propaganda as part of dispute with Parliament leading to the Civil War.

1640 Scots invade England and Charles I is again at York. House of Lords meets in the city.

1644 York, a Royalist stronghold in the Civil War, is surrounded and besieged by Parliamentarians. The city surrenders after the Royalist army is defeated at nearby Marston Moor.

1646 A room in York's Guildhall used by parliamentarian Roundheads to pay out £200,000 to the Scots for the surrender of Charles I.

1706 Stage coaches achieve a regular four-day service between the city and London.

1731–2 Assembly Rooms are built and become a meeting place for smart Georgian society.

1731 First horse races held at Knavesmire.

1735 Dick Turpin, the highwayman, condemned at York Assizes and hanged. His body is stolen by 'resurrection men' and hidden in a garden, before being recovered and re-buried.

1745 After the failure of the Jacobite rebellion public hangings of rebels on Knavesmire become popular entertainment.

1759 Irish novelist Lawrence Sterne becomes member of the York Club which meets in Coney Street Coffee House. He uses many of its members as 'characters' in his writings.

1767 Terry's Confectionery Works established in Clementhorpe.

1800 York's population reaches 16,000.

1807 New prison built at York with a new 'drop' on nearby St George's Field to avoid processions of condemned prisoners through crowded city streets to execution on Knavesmire.

1829 Jonathan Martin hides in York Minster and starts a fire which destroys the choir and the roof. Found guilty but insane, he dies in the madhouse.

1838 Rowntree Works founded in Coppergate.

1840 The first journey by rail from York to London takes 13 hours. New era of travel proclaimed – breakfast in York, tea in the capital. Another fire destroys the nave of Minster.

1845 The racing fraternity at York form the Gimcrack Club and start the Gimcrack Stakes which is still an annual event at York Races.

1849 George Hudson, York's Railway King, disgraced in shares fiasco and his picture is removed from the Mansion House where he had been Lord Mayor.

1856 Complaints about lack of cheap train excursions to York to cope with the huge crowds attending the public hangings on St George's Field.

1877 New railway station – a cathedral to steam, built on a gracious curve – opens at York.

1907 York becomes headquarters of the Army's Northern Command. Population about 51,000.

1916 Zeppelin raids on York.

1942 Baedeker raid by German bombers damages York Station but the Minster escapes.

1951 Festival of Britain. York stages its own festival and revives medieval Mystery Plays after a break of 400 years.

1961 The Duke of Kent marries Miss Katherine Worsley in the Minster in the presence of the Queen and 62 members of the Royal family.

1963 York University founded.

1971 The Queen accompanied by the Household Cavalry visits York for the city's 1900th anniversary celebrations.

1976–81 Archaeologists find remains of Viking York (Jorvik) in excavations in Coppergate. Finds excite worldwide interest and the 'dig' attracts royal visitors from Scandinavia.

1984 Lightning strikes the Minster and fire destroys South Transept roof. Prince Charles officially opens Jorvik Viking Centre built over the Coppergate excavation site.

2005 Archbishop John Sentamu, enthroned in York Minster, becomes the first black archbishop in the Church of England.

2006 The Yorkshire Wheel opens.

14

Bootham

Saint Mary's

Gillygate

Bootham Row

Marygate Tower **12**

City Walls

Minster Library **3**

Sycamore Terrace

Townend Terrace

St Mary's Abbey (ruins) **49**

City Art Gallery **11**

10

Bootham Bar **9**

DEAN'S PARK

Marygate

King's Manor **55**

Exhibition Square

De Grey Rooms

i **56**

York Minster **1**

St Michael-le-Belfry **13**

Frederic Street

St Olave's Church **48**

Yorkshire Museum **52**

St Leonard's Place

High Petergate

Theatre Royal **57**

Twelfth Century House

62

MUSEUM GARDENS

Anglian Tower **54**

Duncombe Pl.

Red House **58**

Old Starre Inn

Minster Gates

Hospitium **50**

Multangular Tower **53**

City Library **59**

Georgian Assembly Rooms

Barley Hall

Grape Lane

River Ouse

Astronomical Observatory **51**

St Leonard's Hospital **60**

15

Stonegate

St Helen's Church **16**

14

Swine

National Railway Museum & Yorkshire Wheel

47

Lendal Tower **35**

Museum Street

Judge's Lodgings

61

St Helen's Square

Lime Stonegate

Davygate

Leeman Road

Station Rise

Barker Tower **36**

Lendal Bridge

Guildhall **18**

Mansion House **17**

New Street

Coney Street

Feasegate

Market St.

Station Street

Station St

Rougier Street

North Street

St Martin-le-Grand **19**

Railway War Memorial **37**

Tanner Row

George Hudson St.

North Street

All Saints **46**

St John Micklegate **45**

Arts Centre

St Michael Spurriergate

Nessgate

York Railway Station **39**

Cholera Burial Ground **38**

Tott Green

Micklegate House **41**

Micklegate

Micklegate

Micklegate

Bridge St.

Ouse Bridge

Queen's Staith

Skeldergate

King's Staith

Grand Opera House **34**

Holy Trinity Church **42**

St Martin-cum-Gregory **44**

Trinity Lane

Jacob's Well **43**

Priory Street

Jewbury

Father Lane

York Dungeon **33**

Queen Street

Micklegate Bar **40**

St Mary's Church

Bishophill

Bishophill South

Buckingham St.

Cinema

The Bar Convent

Nunnery Lane

Lower Priory Street

City Walls

Fairfax Street

Hampden Street

Victor Street

Cromwell Road

Skeldergate

Blossom Street

Newton Terrace

Kyme Street

Baile Hill **88**

Price's Lane

**ROUTES 1–7
YORK CITY CENTRE**

0 ___ 400 m
0 ___ 400 yds

N

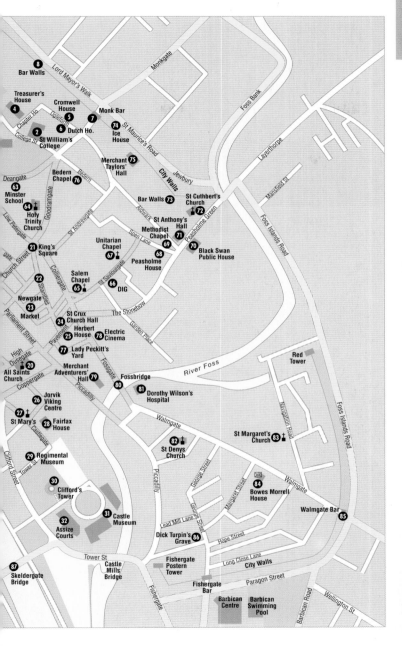

- **8** Bar Walls
- **4** Treasurer's House
- **5** Cromwell House
- **2** St William's College
- **6** Dutch Ho.
- **7** Monk Bar
- **74** St Maurice's Road Ice House
- **75** Merchant Taylors' Hall
- **76** Bedern Chapel
- **63** Minster School
- **64** Holy Trinity Church
- **73** Bar Walls
- **72** St Cuthbert's Church
- **21** King's Square
- **67** Unitarian Chapel
- **69** St Anthony's Hall
- **71** Methodist Chapel
- **68** Peasholme House
- **70** Black Swan Public House
- **22** Collengate
- **65** Salem Chapel
- **66** DIG
- **23** Newgate Market
- **24** St Crux Church Hall
- **25** Herbert House
- **78** Electric Cinema
- **77** Lady Peckitt's Yard
- **20** All Saints Church
- **79** Merchant Adventurers' Hall
- **80** Fossbridge
- **81** Dorothy Wilson's Hospital
- **26** Jorvik Viking Centre
- **27** St Mary's
- **28** Fairfax House
- **82** St Denys Church
- **83** St Margaret's Church
- **29** Regimental Museum
- **30** Clifford's Tower
- **84** Bowes Morrell House
- **31** Castle Museum
- **85** Walmgate Bar
- **32** Assize Courts
- **86** Dick Turpin's Grave
- **87** Skeldergate Bridge
- **Castle Mills Bridge**
- **Fishergate Postern Tower**
- **Fishergate Bar**
- **Barbican Centre**
- **Barbican Swimming Pool**
- **Red Tower**

15

The Minster
Preceding pages:
The National Rail Museum

Route 1

The heart of York

The Minster – St William's College – Minster Library – Treasurer's House – Monk Bar – Bootham Bar – Exhibition Square – York Art Gallery *See map, pages 14–15*

The first route starts at York's fabulous Gothic cathedral, the mother church for England's 'Northern Province', and explores the environs of the Minster, including St William's College and Treasurer's House, before climbing up on to the medieval walls at Monk Bar for a picturesque walk along the ramparts and a semi-aerial view of the old city.

The West Window

★★★ **The Minster** (Mon–Sat 9am–4.45pm, opening at 9.30am Nov–Mar; Sun 12–3.45pm; early services only from 7am; guided tours begin at the Group Desk, admission charges) is the largest Gothic cathedral north of the Alps and is both a cathedral and a minster – a cathedral because of its archbishop's throne and a minster because it has been served since Saxon times by a team of clergy. It has the widest nave in England, stands 196ft (60m) high, is 525ft (160m) long and 250ft (76m) wide across the transepts. Despite its size, recent restorations and cleaning give the visitor an impression of airy lightness. Its dimensions may make an immediate impression, but its ornate detail makes it an attraction worth spending an entire day exploring.

The history of the Minster is the history of England. A Roman legion's headquarters stood here from AD71 before the first wooden church was founded in AD627, followed by two Norman cathedrals. The present Gothic cathedral, completed in 1472, took more than 250 years to build.

There was major restoration after two serious 19th-century fires. In 1829 a religious fanatic, Jonathan Martin, set fire to the choir (quire) area destroying its stalls and roof. A workman's candle set fire to the South West Tower in 1840 and severely damaged the nave. A third fire in 1984 caused, it is thought, by lightning, destroyed the south transept roof. The restored transept was rededicated by the Queen in 1988. Major restoration work was also carried out between 1967 and 1972 when cracks were found in the central tower and other parts of the cathedral were found to be unstable. Repairs involved giving the tower new steel reinforced concrete 'feet', which can be seen in the undercroft.

This is still a living church and regular pauses for prayer are announced over a speaker system. It is also the site for the enthronement of the Archbishop of York. The current Archbishop, John Sentamu, enthroned in November 2005, became the first black archbishop in the Church of England.

Visitors enter via ticket barriers in the South Transept. Anger at the introduction of an entry fee made it all the way to Parliament, where one MP described the imposition as 'tacky'. Nevertheless, claimed church officials, the money for ongoing restorations must be found somewhere.

The Nave

17

One of many fine windows

Begin your tour in the **Nave [A]** to the west (left as you enter). The main body of the Minster is Decorated Gothic in style and was completed in the 1350s. The 14th-century ★ **West Window [B]** painted in 1338 has become known as the 'Heart of Yorkshire' because of the heart shape in the ornate tracery. The stonework became badly eroded and was replaced and rededicated in 1989. The space below the window is now used to exhibit contemporary artworks inspired by the building. Looking upwards, the shields in the arches of the nave are the arms of nobles who fought with Edward I and Edward II against the Scots in the 14th century. The central line of bosses on the roof vaulting portrays scenes from the life of Christ, with one exception. Victorian craftsmen, when called upon to restore the nave after the fire of 1840, replaced the traditional image of the Virgin Mary breast-feeding baby Jesus with

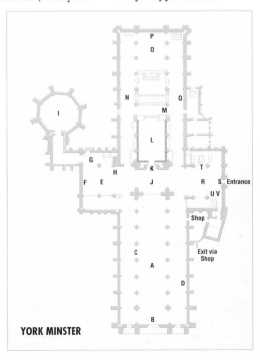

YORK MINSTER

Chapter House ceiling

AS DYING AND BEHOLD WE LIVE

Astronomical Clock

The Screen

one in which he is being bottle fed, leaving the Holy Virgin's modesty safely covered. All the other bosses are exact replicas of their medieval versions. The **Dragon's Head [C]** peeping out from the upper gallery is a crane probably used to lift a font cover. To the right of the nave is the **Jesse Window [D]**, a 1310 version of Jesus's family tree, with the Saviour at the top and his ancestor Jesse at the bottom.

The **North Transept [E]** in Early English style is dominated by the **Five Sisters' Window [F]** (1260), the oldest complete window in the Minster, which is made of green and grey 'grisaille' glass – clear glass etched with fine black lines and set in geometric patterns. The **Astronomical Clock [G]** is a memorial to 18,000 airmen who lost their lives in World War II while flying from airfields in Northern England. At the nearby **Striking Clock [H]**, Gog and Magog, both 400-year-old figures, strike the hours and quarters.

The ★★ **Chapter House [I]** off the corner of the transept is regarded as the architectural wonder of its age. The beautiful domed roof of the octagonal building is not supported by a central pillar. Around the walls are canopied stalls with some of the world's finest medieval carvings, many of them laced with wit and humour. The titles in the arched seats denote members of the College of Canons, which meets to decide important issues regarding the Minster.

The **Central Tower and Crossing [J]** is Perpendicular in style with the ceiling's central carving depicting St Peter and St Paul. The **Screen [K]** is decorated with the statues of 15 kings of England from William I to Henry VI all edged with gold and against a scarlet background.

The **Choir [L]** is the focal point of worship in the Minster where daily services are held. It was originally built to prevent 'unprepared' laity from seeing the mass. The ornate stalls are copies of those destroyed in the fire started by Jonathan Martin. It is from here that evensong is sung

most days. To the right is the Archbishop's **Throne [M]**, or *cathedra*. Leaving the choir by the left exit, there is the **St William Window** (1422) **[N]** showing scenes from the life of Archbishop William Fitzherbert (d. 1154) whose shrine stood near the High Altar until the Reformation. The **Lady Chapel [O]** in the east end is often used for Holy Communion services. The ★ **Great East Window [P]** above it contains the world's largest area of medieval stained glass in a single window and stands 76ft (23m) high and 32ft (10m) wide. In 1405 a Coventry glazier, John Thornton, started work on the window and completed the task in the contract-agreed three years. He received four shillings a week and £10 on completion. The window's theme is the beginning and the end of the world using scenes from the Bible. God the Father is at the apex reading from a book: '*Ego Sum Alpha et Omega* ...' Much of the eastern facade is undergoing restoration for the next couple of years.

The Five Sisters

On the south side of the choir, the **St Cuthbert Window** (1435) **[Q]** shows scenes from the saint's life.

The ★ **South Transept [R]**, where you entered the Minster, was restored after the fire in 1984 and the new ceiling has become a major tourist attraction. Mirrored tables save the neck muscles when examining the superbly carved and decorated new ceiling bosses. All but six of the original carvings were destroyed in the fire. Among the 68 new carvings depicting significant events of the 20th century are six designed by winners of a competition held by children's television programme *Blue Peter*. The ★ **Rose Window [S]** narrowly escaped destruction in the 1984 fire but had to be dismantled and strengthened before being replaced. The red and white roses in the design commemorate the ending of the Wars of the Roses with the wedding in 1486 of King Henry VII and Elizabeth of York – a wedding which also marked the beginning of the Tudor dynasty. Against the east wall of the south transept is the **Tomb of Archbishop de Gray [T]**. Much of the present Minster was his vision and design. During restoration of his tomb a painting of him was discovered on the coffin lid beneath his marble effigy.

The Rose Window

Entrance to the ★ **Undercroft, Treasury and Crypt [U]** is via a staircase in the South Transept (admission charge, no disabled access). It contains the concrete 'feet' of the Central Tower which now have stainless steel bolts to reinforce them and were designed to stop the feared collapse of the tower in 1967. There are also the walls of former Norman churches on the site and beneath these the remains of the Roman fortress – set at an angle to the Christian alignment of the buildings above. Painted plaster work from one of the Roman rooms has been reconstructed. The Treasury has a glittering collection of silver plate including the 11th-century Horn of Ulf, a gift from a Viking thane, and a 13th-

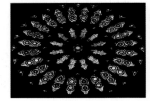

*St William's College
from inside and out*

century Heart Casket which probably belonged to a crusader. The mysterious York Virgin was found after the fire in 1829 and could date back to the 10th century and be the only remaining fragment of the Saxon Minster.

There are 275 spiralling stone steps to the top of the ★ **Central Tower Roof [V]** (admission charge). The view is magnificent but the climb can be claustrophobic and is not advisable for the unfit.

Leave the cathedral via the gift shop and follow the path alongside the cathedral to the left known as Queen's Path since Queen Elizabeth II took this route to the Treasurer's House after distributing the Royal Maundy money in 1972.

Ahead is the half-timbered **St William's College ❷**. The college has been turned into the Minster's Visitors' Centre in an effort to cope with the millions of tourists the city receives every year.

St William's was founded in 1461 as the home of chantry priests – priests who said mass in the cathedral for those who had given endowments to the chantry. With the Dissolution of the Monasteries in 1536–39, the priests were ordered out and the building passed into private hands, most notably those of Charles I; he set up a printing press here in 1641, firing off 'paper bullets' in his propaganda war against Parliament. In 1906 it was sold back to the church and became the meeting place for the bishops and clergy of the Northern Province in the Convocation of York until 1959. Its courtyard is now part of St William's College Restaurant – a very pleasant place to take a break after your Minster tour *(see page 68)*

Turn right on leaving St William's and walk along the northern side of the Minster and its Chapter House into **Dean's Park** to see the ★ **Minster Library ❸** (Mon–Thur 9am–5pm, Fri 9am–12pm). This is housed in the former 13th-century private chapel of the Archbishop's Palace

Young visitor to Dean's Park

which once covered this area. The Library – the largest cathedral library in the country – has at its core the books of Archbishop Matthew, who died in 1628, supplemented by later donations of books and manuscripts. An extension in 1998 allowed space for a modern reading room and conservation space for older documents such as the library's 115 items that date back to before 1500. The library also provides a biographical database for those studying their family trees and hosts temporary exhibits from its archives. Near the library is the only other remnant of the Archbishop's Palace – the arcading now called the Kohima Memorial.

Return by the same route, looking through a gateway into the walled garden of the **Treasurer's House** ❹ (Mar–Nov 11am–4.30pm; garden, tea room and gallery free). Built in 1419, probably as the home of a Minster treasurer, the house has passed through many hands over the years and has had any number of changes and additions. It was from here that John Goodricke, the 18th-century astronomer, made his observations. Francis William Green, a Wakefield engineer, extensively restored the house between 1897 and 1900 and filled it with the antique furniture which is on view today. The National Trust took over the house in 1930 including its cohort of ghosts. They were seen, it is claimed, by a workman doing repairs in the cellar. Roman legionnaires marched through one wall and out through the other but all of them cut off at the knees; a Roman road runs a few feet below the cellar floor. Entrance to the house is by guided tour only.

Treasurer's House

Monk Bar

From Treasurer's House turn left into cobbled Chapter House Street, where the cottages have overhanging upper storeys, and into Ogleforth, probably named after a Dane called Ugel. At No. 13 is **Cromwell House** ❺ built about 1700. Opposite and isolated by the demolition of surrounding property is the curious brick-built **Dutch House** ❻ erected in 1660. Fear of fire among half-timbered structures after the Great Fire of London is thought to have prompted this type of fire-resistant construction, and a lack of local knowledge about small-scale brick building could have forced craftsmen into borrowing a Dutch pattern.

Continue into Goodramgate to **Monk Bar** ❼ and on to the ★★★ **Bar Walls** ❽. The bar or gateway has four storeys and dates from the 14th century with the coat of arms of the Plantagenets adorning the external face. The parapets have statues of defenders about to hurl stones on attackers. They would fool no one in daytime but might have made night-time raiders nervous. In the 16th century the rooms were used as a prison. It's now the rather grim **Richard III Museum** (Mar–Oct 9am–5pm, Nov–Feb 9.30am–4pm, admission charge) offering guests the chance to be the Jury at his trial, relive the executions he ordered when king

The Bar Walls

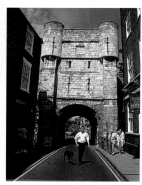

Bootham Bar

City Art Gallery and detail above

and operate a portcullis. In August the upper rooms host performances of *An Audience with Richard III*.

From here begins a panoramic view of the city looking across pantiled roofs and gardens to the cathedral and over the Georgian homes in its precincts. One can look down on the gardens of **Grays Court**, where the Royalists held their Civil War battle conferences, and peep into the Dean's garden behind the Minster. Much of this area was occupied by the 12th- and 13th-century Archbishop's Palace, only fragments of which remain.

Outside the ramparts runs a deep ditch – all that remains of a moat that once defended the city. In the spring the grass banks are speckled with daffodils but it was not always so pleasant. The Canons of York Minster had their privies along these banks and the city's butchers tossed their offal over the walls into the water. Records from the 15th century describe plagues of flies and vermin and a 'great corruption and horrible and pernicious air.'

The wall does a sharp right-angled turn and runs in a southwesterly direction behind houses in Gillygate while overlooking, on the left, the private Purey Cust Nursing Home. Leave the wall at **Bootham Bar** ❾ which has its portcullis permanently lifted and provides an archer's view through the arrow slits of High Petergate and Bootham. The view outwards was once straight into the vast Forest of Galtres. Armed guards waited in the bar to act as guides through the dangerous woods and to protect travellers from packs of wolves. Traitors heads were spiked here. The bar's barbican was removed in 1832 and the gateway itself was only saved from demolition after strong public protests.

Descend into **Exhibition Square** ❿ with its attractive fountain and statue of William Etty, York's most famous artist. He was much abused in his lifetime for his paintings of nudes, but his work dominates the English paintings in the ★ ★ **City Art Gallery** ⓫ (daily 9.30am–4.30pm). The gallery also has many Old Masters on view, including the F.D. Lycett Green collection of European art which he donated in 1955, and regularly hosts temporary exhibitions.

From Exhibition Square you can see the jagged end of the defensive wall of St Mary's Abbey, torn down at this point in the early 19th century to make way for a new road into the city. It continues up Bootham, where houses have been built against it, to **Marygate Tower** ⓬. This was blown up by the Parliamentarians during the Civil War. They burst in only to be thrown out with heavy losses.

The wall turns at this point and goes down to the river, enclosing the Museum Gardens covered in Route 5 (*see page 41*).

Route 2

Shopping streets

Bootham Bar – High Petergate – Stonegate – Assembly Rooms – St Helen's Church – Mansion House – Guildhall – Coney Street – St Martin-le-Grand – All Saints, Pavement – Parliament Street *See map, pages 14–15*

Bootham Bar plaque

This route takes in the main shopping streets of York, its administrative headquarters, the centre of the old coaching trade and some of its ancient churches.

Bootham Bar *(see opposite page)* stands on the western entrance to Roman York, the Prima Porta Dextra. High Petergate heads for the centre of town following the line of the old Roman Via Principia. The street was described as one of 'squalor and congestion' in early medieval times with booths narrowing the thoroughfare. Today it is smart and attractive but still narrow until it suddenly opens out to an imposing view of the cathedral's twin-towered West Front. When Charles I visited the city the West Front was obscured by a row of cottages and there were houses built along the west and south side of the cathedral, some actually leaning against it. The king protested but it was not until 1702, when the last of the leases expired, that the Minster authorities had them pulled down. In the 19th century the narrow Lop Lane was widened to become Duncombe Place, opening out the present fine view of the cathedral.

23

St Michael-le-Belfry 🔞 gets its name from the nearby belfry of the Minster and has in its register the christening of one Guy Fawkes, son of Edward Fawkes, April 16, 1570 – the man who tried to blow up Parliament. There are claims that Guy was born just across the road in what was Young's Hotel, but it is more likely that his home was in Stonegate *(see page 24)*.

Minerva

A passage in the life of St John of Beverley suggests a very early foundation date for St Michael's, but the present church was built between 1525 and 1536 and contains no earlier features.

At the end of **High Petergate**, at Minster Gates looking towards the South Door of the cathedral, is **Minerva**, goddess of wisdom, leaning on a pile of books in an elegant carving above a corner shop. This is a legacy of a time when this part of the city was dominated by the book trade.

Stonegate

At this point turn right into ★★★ **Stonegate** 🔞, the finest street in York. The former 15th- and 16th-century houses have been converted into high-quality shops set behind

Beautiful cakes at Little Betty's

Coffee Yard

Barley Hall

elegant Victorian and Georgian shop facades. Again the Romans got here first – it was their Via Praetoria. During excavation work on the street below the present surface the grooves of chariot wheels were found. The present name means 'stone paved' but this was also the route taken by the Minster masons when hauling their stone to the cathedral site from the river.

A doorway labelled Stonegate Gallery (52A) on the right leads to the remains of the oldest house in the city, now just two walls of a small courtyard. The **Norman House** was built about 1180 and is thought to have been used by the clergy.

A large sign has hung across the street since 1753 pointing down an alleyway to the ★ **Olde Starre Inne** set in its own courtyard and mentioned by name in a Civil War pamphlet of 1644. Nearby is Little Betty's Café. Its fine cakes and gourmet coffees are the sophisticate's answer to the morning after the night before.

Leading off Stonegate to the left is **Coffee Yard**, so called since the coffee houses became popular meeting places in the city. The Irish author Laurence Sterne was a frequent visitor to what he called these 'chit chat' clubs. He 'flirted' with Kitty, a professional singer who lived in the street, and the first edition of his book *Tristram Shandy* was published in 1759 by John Hinxmana, a bookseller in Stonegate. The city's first newspaper was printed here too, which explains the carved red printer's devil at the entrance to Coffee Yard (the 'devils' were the young boys who carried the type).

Down the yard is ★ **Barley Hall** (Mar–Oct Tues–Sun 10am–4pm, Nov–Feb 12–4pm), the home of Alderman William Snawsell, a 15th-century goldsmith. His house has been refurbished by the Barley Hall Trust and is filled with furniture and fittings made by modern craftsmen to recreate the life of a merchant's house. Many of the exhibits are hands on and special events, such as Viking markets and medieval fayres, are held throughout the year.

Among the shops in Stonegate is **Mulberry Hall**, a 15th-century bishop's town house now selling porcelain and serving tea upstairs. Outside No. 32 is a second reference to Guy Fawkes – the rebel's parents are believed to have lived 'hereabouts'. On a 17th-century half-timbered shop corner leading into Little Stonegate is a carving of a **topless angel** taken from the prow of a ship. Frequently battered by lorries before the days of pedestrianisation, she has been restored and now faces a more tranquil future.

Nestling among the shops is one of the oldest pubs in York, the 17th-century **Old Punch Bowl Inn**. It was here that members of the Gimcrack Club held their annual lunches with the winner of the Gimcrack Stakes on Knavesmire having to provide three dozen bottles of Champagne for the festivities. The Stakes are still run and the Club meets annually, but these days at the racecourse.

Another narrow passage on the right leads to Stonegate Alley, a narrow lane with a couple of modern shops. Continue down Stonegate to the entrance of St Helen's Square and turn right into Blake Street. On the left are the **Georgian Assembly Rooms** ⑮. This was the place for fashionable assemblies and balls even though Sarah, Duchess of Marlborough, complained that the space between the pillars was too narrow for her hooped skirts. Lord Burlington's hall has been likened to an Egyptian temple with the roof supported by double rows of pillars, 52 in all, decorated with painted yellow and brown marbling and topped by Corinthian style capitals picked out in gold, green and purple. Burlington's brief was to provide a dancing room of not less than 90ft (27m) long and ancillary rooms for cards and refreshments. His design was influential and the Rooms were hailed as his masterpiece. The cost was borne by public subscription and the Rooms were ready for the race week of August 1732.

Royalty, nobility and famous beauties patronised the dances – the King of Denmark in 1768 and the Duke of York in 1761 as well as the northern aristocracy. But towards the end of the century the fashion for balls and assemblies waned and the building struggled to find a continuous use. The 1951 Festival of Britain saw it restored and used for dances including a Georgian Ball attended by descendants of the families who had paid the original subscriptions. It remained in irregular use for social functions until, unbelievably, it was deemed to have no better function than as home to a chain pizzeria with a far less grand dress code.

The Red Devil of Stonegate

25

Mulberry Hall, Stonegate

Stained glass in St Helen's

Glass painter's coat of arms

*Mansion House
dressed for Christmas*

Return down Blake Street and into St Helen's Square overlooked by the Mansion House and more fashionable tea rooms. One of them, **Betty's**, with a downstairs bar, was a favourite meeting place for off-duty World War II flyers from the nearby bomber airfields. The mirror on which many scratched their names has been preserved.

Tucked in the corner of the square opposite is **St Helen's Church** 🔟 where the Lord Mayor and corporation attend Harvest Thanksgiving every year. It is convenient for the Mansion House across the square and took over as the city civic church when St Martin's in Coney Street was destroyed in an air raid in 1942. St Helen's narrowly escaped destruction itself in 1552 when it was sold off by the corporation and partly demolished. A local action group was formed and parishioners successfully protested that its loss from the square 'defaced and deformed' the city. It was rebuilt under Crown patronage.

Glass painters associated with the Minster lived in this area and have the **coat of arms** of their guild in the west window of the south aisle. The church lies at the entrance to Davygate, a name taken from Davy Hall, now demolished, which comes in turn from David the Lardener. His family, which can be traced back as far as the early 12th century, inherited the responsibility for keeping the king's larder at York stocked with food, including game, and domestic animals. In return he received land, rights and privileges which the family duly exercised for more than 200 years. But they ended up in court when there were mutterings about extortion, and citizens questioned the family's right to take tolls in cash and kind from every food shop in the city.

The ★ **Mansion House** 🔟 (tours Mar–Dec Fri and Sat at 11am and 2pm) is the residence of the city's Lord Mayor during his term of office as First Citizen. The house was completed in 1730, 10 years before London's Lord Mayor had his Mansion House. The City Arms adorn the pediment and in summer, with the window boxes in flower and with its ornate black and gilded railings and lamp-posts sparkling, the building looks as pretty as a doll's house.

To be admired inside the building are the fine state rooms and a superb collection of civic plate and regalia which includes a 15th-century sword which belonged to the Holy Roman Emperor Sigismund. An ermine-trimmed scarlet Cap of Maintenance was presented to the city by Richard II with the privilege of wearing it before Royalty. New caps were bought in 1445 and 1580 and this last cap is still in existence. The latest cap, acquired in 1915, is worn by the Lord Mayor's attendant on civic occasions. There is also a Great Mace dated 1657 (at one time the Lord Mayor had six mace bearers) and a gold chain of office made in 1647.

Mansion House detail

Now follow the arched passageway alongside the Mansion House to arrive at the ★ **Guildhall** ⓰. Note the hooks in the ceiling under the archway, which were used to hang game and meat, as a cool larder for the First Citizen's house next door. Underneath the whole complex and reached through an iron gateway (in the wall on the right) a damp passageway runs down to a small quay on the Ouse. It was much used in times when transport by water was safer than by road, and indeed one particularly enterprising Lord Mayor revived its use in recent times. He kept a skiff in the passageway so that he could take a regular row on the river.

Guildhall memorial

The Guildhall at the bottom of the courtyard was first mentioned in 1256 but rebuilt and enlarged in the 15th century. Since 1810 the city's business has been conducted from here using a council chamber rich with Victorian carved seating and desks and with windows overlooking the river. Committee Room No. 1 (complete with secret panel) is where the Scots received payment in silver from the Parliamentarians in 1646 for handing over Charles I who had fled to Scotland. The cash was counted out on the table.

Decoration in the Common Hall

The large **Common Hall** is a replica: the original building was destroyed in an air raid in 1942. Pillars, each made from a single oak tree, support an arch-braced roof with decorated bosses. A magnificent modern stained-glass west window was added during rebuilding. Designed by York artist Harry Harvey, it continues the city's long tradition of glass painting showing scenes and characters from York's past. The hall is now used for a variety of exhibitions as well as meetings.

Turn along **Coney Street** (a corruption of the Danish for King's Street) and into the city's busy main shop-

St Martin-le-Grand's
'Little Admiral'

Restored sculpture

ping area. Most of the original properties have been destroyed and there is little to see of old Coney Street but much to find in the history books. Where tradition has perished, modern commerce has thrived and this is now one of York's most popular shopping streets *(see page 68 for futher details)*.

Here, though, is what remains of the church of ★ **St Martin-le-Grand** ⑲ after it was fire-bombed during World War II. Some of the church's stained glass was blown out and sank into the tar of the road which had become molten in the inferno. Still proudly 'shooting the sun' with his sextant is the 'Little Admiral', a 17th-century carved figure above the church clock. The admiral had his coat tails badly singed in the same fire. He returned repaired and repainted to stand on top of the huge clock which hangs above the pavement on its cast-iron brackets. St Martin's was one of the city's finest parish churches and it has been partially restored, its open south aisle being dedicated to all those citizens of York who sacrificed their lives in World War II. The restoration work has preserved the former southwest tower and the area around the south door. A large 15th-century stained-glass window, which had been removed for safekeeping before the war, has been returned and there is, moreover, a modern stained-glass window that illustrates the church on fire. Not far away you will find an organ presented to St Martin's by the German government.

A plaque on a wall by the Yorkshire Bank marks the site of the Black Swan Inn and is the only visible clue to what Coney Street once was – the thriving centre for the city's long-distance coach trade. Coaches leaving the two coaching inns in Coney Street in 1706 took 96 hours to reach the capital. In 1774 a 'flying coach' clipped the time to 36 hours; in 1818 the special express mail coaches were doing the journey in 29 hours and eventually got the trip down to only 20 hours in 1836. The Great North Mail service passed through Coney Street but in 1820 the city was up in arms after attempts were made to speed up the London to Edinburgh mail by cutting out York. The city protested and kept its fast link 'up to town'.

There is, however, no marker for another famous Coney Street coaching inn, the George, at which Sir John Vanburgh stayed while supervising the building of Castle Howard *(see page 57)*. Somewhere in this street, too, lived Aaron of York, the greatest of all the 13th-century Anglo-Jewish financiers. He is said to have financed a loan for building the Five Sisters Window in the Minster before he was cheated by Henry III and reduced to penury.

All Saints Church

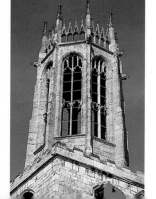

Continue past the shops into Spurriergate and turn left into High Ousegate to ★ ★ **All Saints Church, Pavement** ⑳. This church is very ancient, for it was mentioned in the

Domesday Book (1086) and has a 13th-century doom or sanctuary **knocker** on the door showing a bearded sinner being eaten by a lion. A fugitive laying hold of the door knob could claim sanctuary from his pursuers, which he maintained until he came out again. Another of the church's claims to fame is the unusual open-top lantern tower. A lantern has hung here since medieval times so that travellers passing through the nearby dark Forest of Galtres could see in which direction the city lay.

The light still shines, but as a war memorial. The church has been pinched by busy roads. In the 17th century the churchyard to the north and south was taken for street widening and in 1782 the chancel was demolished so the market in Pavement could be made larger. No fewer than 39 Lord Mayors are buried in the church which still has strong links with the Corporation. The surviving city guilds process in their robes to this church for annual services.

Now turn left into **Parliament Street** past what locals call the 'splash palace' – a former Victorian public convenience restored, enlarged and decorated with a gabled roof and clock tower to become a truly modern 'comfort station' complete with an office for the City Centre Manager in the roof space. Parliament Street has recently been transformed into a delightful Yorkshire version of a French town square. The area has been paved and planted with plane trees, decorated with a fountain and set out with seats which attract crowds of visitors and locals to watch the street entertainers during the summer. This broad open space was created in 1836 by knocking down old property to allow the overcrowded market in Pavement to expand. The market, however, has since contracted and been moved into Newgate *(see page 30).*

Festive spirit, Parliament Street

All Saints: the doom knocker

29

All Saints interior

Morris dancers in Parliament Street

Route 3

Markets and museums

**King's Square – The Shambles – Pavement – Jorvik
Viking Centre – St Mary's, Castlegate – Fairfax House
– Clifford's Tower – Castle Museum – York Dungeon
– The Grand Opera House** *See map, pages 14–15*

This route starts in the busy heart of the city and takes
in most of the city centre museums and markets.

The Shambles

★ **King's Square ㉑** is the place to be in summer, particularly at lunch time. Jugglers, acrobats and pavement artists provide some of the best busking entertainment in the north of England. A Royal Viking court is
thought to be responsible for the name but the square
only came into existence in 1937 when the ancient
church of Holy Trinity, King's Court. was pulled down.
Old tombstones from the graveyard are set into the
square's pavements.

★★★ **The Shambles ㉒** starts in the southeast corner
of the square and gives an immediate impression of what
York must have looked like in Elizabethan times but
without the squalor and the smells. This is one of the best
preserved and oldest medieval streets in the whole of Europe. Once called Fleshammels (the street of the butchers) the broad window sills are a legacy of the shelves on
which meat was displayed.

The half-timbered houses lean inwards and neigh-
bours could shake hands with each other across the
street. The butchers' shops have long gone. Instead there
are gift and craft shops and the only odours (all pleasant)
come from a pizza restaurant. The old **Butchers' Hall** is
at No. 40. At No. 35 there is a shrine to **Margaret
Clitherow**, the butcher's wife who was pressed to death
in 1586 for harbouring Jesuit priests. She was canonised
as St Margaret of York in 1970.

Three narrow alleyways on the right lead into the
Newgate Market ㉓, open daily with stalls selling
everything from fish to fashions. York's medieval markets were so famous and grew so large that city centre
property had to be demolished to accommodate them
(see Parliament Street, page 29). It is much more modest
now, but Henshelwood's Delicatessen is one of many
fine food shops still trading here.

Newgate Market

At the end of the street on the left is **St Crux Church
Hall ㉔** (there is no Saint Crux – the name means Holy
Cross). What was once the finest medieval church in York
was declared unsafe and demolished in 1887 and the
church hall built from the stones. Inside are some of the

memorials from the original church. The hall is now the parish room of All Saints, Pavement.

Pavement – the first paved street in the city – was the main market area, the place for executions and where 'minor' punishments such as whippings and pillorying took place. Overlooking the street is the richly carved ★ **Herbert House** , the finest black- and-white half-timbered building in the city. Christopher Herbert, Lord Mayor of London, bought a house on this site in 1557 and the present town house was built about 1620. His great grandson, Sir Thomas Herbert, was born here and as valet to Charles I attended the king on his way to execution.

Survivors from St Crux

Turning right towards the tower of All Saints, Pavement *(see page 28)* and passing it on the right, turn left into a new street, Coppergate Walk. This was the site of a sweet factory before it became an archaeological dig frequently visited by British and Scandinavian royalty in the late 1970s. It was here that the wooden house walls and wicker fences of Viking Jorvik were discovered standing shoulder high.

On the spot where they were found (beneath the new shops) the discoveries have been 'interpreted' in the highly popular ★ ★ ★ **Jorvik Viking Centre**  (daily 10am– 5pm, admission charge). Opened by Prince Charles in 1984, this popular attraction was recently rebuilt in the light of a further 20 years' research into the Viking city that was found on the site. 'Time cars' still whisk visitors back to a reconstructed Viking world which now displays the life and smells of the Viking city with greater authenticity. Market craftsmen are at work and characters chatter at you in old Norse as you pass. Studies of plant and animal remains in the original dig threw new light on the diet and hygiene of the inhabitants of this huge Viking town as they set about the more peaceful occupations of farming and trade. The

31

Jorvik: a meeting with Vikings

The spire of St Mary's

time car ride ends in a gallery filled with exhibits of finds and explains archaeological techniques. During peak periods, it's advisable to book your time car ride in advance as the wait can be quite long (tel: 01904 543 402).

A new, revisionist image of the Vikings emerges, but it is the established reputation of rapists and pillagers that probably attracts the crowds. This rough and ready image still dominates Jorvik's annual Viking festival (Feb), which features more battles than boar roasting.

Not far away is **St Mary's, Castlegate** ㉗. This predominantly 15th-century building was declared redundant in 1958 and was bought by the city council for a nominal five pence in 1972. It has the tallest spire in York at 152ft (46m) high, and is now used to house an annual site-specific installation from the City Art Gallery.

Fairfax House: the lounge

Continue along Castlegate towards Clifford's Tower and on the left is **Fairfax House** ㉘ (Mon–Thur and Sat 11am–4.30pm, Sun 1.30–4.30pm; guided tours Fri at 11am and 2pm; admission charge). One of the finest Georgian houses in England, it was rescued from decay by the York Civic Trust. John Carr built it in 1755–56 for Viscount Fairfax and it has been refurbished to make it look very much as the Viscount would have known it. The furniture was donated by Noel Terry, the great grandson of the founder of the Terry confectionery business in York. The house keeps a full calendar, hosting plays, talks and exhibitons.

Next door is the facade of the former **St George's Cinema** – a Greek style entrance created in 1911 and now regarded as a piece of early 20th-century architectural history in its own right.

Regimental uniform

In Tower Street is the **Regimental Museum** ㉙ of the 4th and 7th Royal Dragoon Guards and the Prince of Wales' Own Regiment of Yorkshire (Mon–Sat 9.30am–4.30pm, admission charge). The museum has displays of regimental colours, uniforms, medals and models of battles fought all over the world by the two regiments.

The huge mound facing the visitor at the end of Castlegate and topped by ★ **Clifford's Tower** ㉚ was hurriedly thrown up by William the Conqueror two years after the Battle of Hastings to keep the north country under control.

Clifford's Tower

The northern English, helped by the Danes, burned down the wooden castle on the mound within a year. Another wooden keep was built during William's 'harrowing of the north' but was burned down again in anti-Jewish riots in 1190 when some 150 Jews lost their lives. There is a plaque to their memory at the foot of the mound.

The stone tower, completed in 1270, was heavily fortified and then wrecked in 1684 when a fire – some say started deliberately – set off the powder magazine and blew off the roof, leaving the structure as it is today. The tower is not yet safe though, developers want to build Coppergate II – a shopping centre, which would surround the tower.

The tower's name might well have derived from the powerful Clifford family, hereditary constables in the area, or it could be a reference to Sir Richard Clifford, who was hanged there in 1322 after a failed rebellion.

One of York citizens' earliest attempts at conservation came in 1596 when Robert Redhead, a jailer, began to pull down the tower intending to burn the masonry for lime. He was stopped after petitions to the government claiming that the tower was 'an especial ornament for the beautifying of this city'. There are information panels inside the tower and a good view of the city from the rampart walk (Apr–Sept 10am–6pm, Oct until 5pm, Nov–Mar until 4pm, admission charge).

Beyond the tower mound can be seen what 18th-century travellers regarded as 'the finest gaol in Britain if not in Europe'. The Debtors' Prison now houses the city's ★★★ Castle Museum ③ (Apr–Oct daily 9.30am–5.30pm, Nov–Mar until 4.30pm, admission charge). The folk museum sprang from a collection of 'everyday things' gathered together by Dr John Kirk, a Pickering country doctor, during his rounds in rural North Yorkshire. He saw a way of life slowly disappearing and was determined to keep mementoes of its passing. In 1938 the City Council installed his collection in the Female Prison, the building on the left.

The covered courtyard became the impressive **Kirkgate**, a cobbled street created from 19th-century shopfronts and filled with the samples of Victoriana collected by the doctor. A fire station, a candle factory and a post office have been re-created and there is a hansom cab waiting in the street. The museum eventually expanded in 1952 into the Debtors' Prison next door and the old prison cells were turned into craft workshops; the Exercise Yard became an Edwardian street with a garage and a pub – again using original building fronts and fittings.

Dick Turpin's cell is here. In 1735 the infamous highwayman was sentenced next door in the Assize Courts and was hanged on St George's Field. On other floors of the old prison are farm implement displays, costumes, weapons and armour and 'period' rooms showing everyday life up to the 1950s.

The 'new' **Assize Courts** ③, which extend like a wing from one side of the Debtors' Prison, were built in the years 1773–77. The Courts, which were designed by John Carr, have an Ionic pillared entrance and a figure of Justice carrying scales and a spear on the roof. Restoration work revealed that Justice had not always been even handed – her scales had been balanced with small coins put into

Vintage items for sale at Kirkgate

33

Kirkgate in the Castle Museum

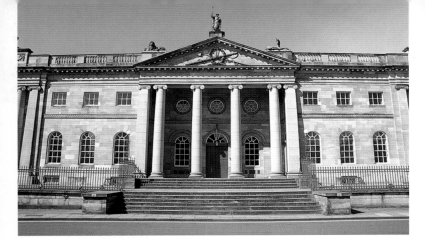

The Assize Courts

York Dungeon: lighting the fuse

The Grand Opera House

the weighing cups. Courts still sit in the two Georgian courtrooms, each set beneath an ornately decorated dome. Apart from Dick Turpin's, the famous trials held here have included such social *causes célèbres* as the Luddites in 1812 and the Peterloo rioters in 1820.

Together with the museum the buildings constitute three sides of a square. Between them lies a sizeable grassed area, much used for picnics, and called the Eye of Yorkshire. County elections used to be held here, proclamations were read, and prisoners executed. What so impressed the Georgians was the spaciousness of the exercise yard in front of the Debtors' Prison where prisoners could walk and talk to friends through the yard railings. A verse scratched on the yard wall is preserved behind glass:

This prison is a house of care, a grave for man alive
A touchstone to try a friend, no place for man to thrive.

The poet was Thomas Smith, aged 28, who was imprisoned here for sheep stealing and hanged in 1820.

Going down the hill to Clifford Street turn right. The **York Dungeon** ❸ (Apr–Sept daily 10.30–5pm; Oct, Feb and Mar until 4.30pm; Nov–Jan 11am–4pm) is the city's own chamber of horrors – complete with blood, groans and mutilations. The **Grand Opera House** ❹ opened in 1902 as a music hall rival to the Theatre Royal. It was designed by the London theatre architect John Briggs. It 'went dark' in 1956, re-opened in 1956 for roller skating, dancing and bingo, and after another period of gloom it is again operating as a theatre.

Walk down the street on the left to King's Staith where, in summer, picnic tables are set out on the river bank in front of the King's Arms. This frequently-photographed pub often features in the news when flood water from the Ouse invades its cellars and drinking areas.

Route 4

An aerial view of railway history

Lendal Bridge – Lendal Tower – City Walls – Micklegate Bar – Micklegate – Holy Trinity Church – Jacob's Well – St Martin cum Gregory – St John Micklegate – Ouse Bridge – All Saints, North Street
See map, pages 14–15

This route starts on a bridge, with a walk along the walls, looking down on scenes of the city's railway history; it then returns along York's old main road from London, taking in medieval churches and another bridge on the way.

Lendal Bridge was built in 1863 to cope with the extra traffic attracted to the city's first railway station which had been built south of the river just inside the bar walls. Previously there had only been a ferry at this point. Tolls were imposed on the new bridge until 1894 to pay for the cost.

Lendal Bridge and Tower views

★ **Lendal Tower** ❸❺ on the north bank – once part of the city's medieval defences – was in 1677 given to a London businessman on a 500-year lease and for a peppercorn rent on condition he supplied piped water to the city within three years. He did so through pipes made of hollowed out elm tree trunks – each half of the city getting water for three days a week in turn. During assizes and busy race weeks water carriers were drafted in to supply the whole city. It has now been recently redeveloped with plans to open it as a boutique hotel and restaurant.

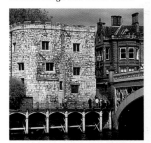
City Walls and the Barker Tower

Cross to the south side of the river where the medieval ★★ **City Walls** start again from **Barker Tower** ❸❻ on the river bank. A chain once hung between the two towers so that waterborne traders could not avoid tolls. Barker Tower was used as a mortuary in the 19th century for bodies recovered from the river. More recently it has been used for stores and a craft shop.

The walls run southwards from here following the line of the defences which the Romans put around their civil settlement. Walk along the parapet over the top of the busy road leading to the station and below to the left is the white obelisk on the **Railway War Memorial** ❸❼ commemorating the 2,236 men of the North Eastern Railway who died in World War I. Behind the memorial are the headquarters offices of the North Eastern Railway, built in 1906. Outside the wall is an area of grass, trees and gravestones – the **Cholera Burial Ground** ❸❽ where victims of an epidemic in 1832 are interred. Superstitious fears of reawakening the disease are said to have preserved the area from later development.

Looking back along the parapet there is the famous picture post card view of York Minster across the river. Look-

Railway Station roof and supports

36

Micklegate Bar

ing out of the city there is one of the city's finest Victorian buildings, the **Royal York**, formerly the Station Hotel.

Below is York's 'new' ★★ **Railway Station** ❸❾ built in 1877 and regarded as one of the finest examples of Victorian railway architecture. The plain brick entrance belies the magnificence within – a gracefully curved 'train shed' covering four lines of through traffic with the curved roof supported on iron Corinthian pillars.

The roof arches are pierced with quatrefoil patterns and the spandrels decorated with the Rose of York and the coats of arms of the three companies who amalgamated to form the North Eastern Railway in 1853. A Victorian shareholder called the station a 'splendid monument of extravagance'. A £900,000 refurbishment of the entrance area was completed in 1984 giving the outer concourse a more welcoming appearance and adding as a decorative feature an old North Eastern Railway semaphore signal. The station is now a listed building.

York's first railway station was a temporary affair sited outside the medieval wall near where it turns at a right angle. This station was quickly found to be inadequate so an archway was punched through the city ramparts (which you walk over) and the railway line came under the walls to a purpose-built station inside – an area now occupied by offices. These were the golden days of York's Lord Mayor and railway 'king', George Hudson, whose proud boast was to 'mak' all railways cum t'York.' The new Lendal Bridge and a new road, George Hudson Street, helped more and more railway passengers to get to his station but the site was too cramped. The terminus was moved back outside the walls to the 'new' station on its present site. Although George Hudson fell into disgrace in a shares scandal, York continued to be a geographical and administrative focal point for railways. Under the wall and earth mound at this point was a railway control room for keeping the region's railways running during World War II. It came into its own when the station was badly bombed during the Baedeker raid on the city in 1942.

Leave the rampart walk at the Royal entry point to the city, ★ **Micklegate Bar** ❹❿. The imposing southern entrance to the city was built in the 12th–14th centuries, probably over an ancient track from the south leading down to the River Ouse. A succession of kings and queens of England have traditionally entered York at this point. Although restored in 1737, the barbican – two protective walls extending in front of the gate – was pulled down in 1839 despite the protests of Sir Walter Scott. His offer to walk from Edinburgh to York if the council would change their minds went unheeded. This was another gateway which was often 'decorated' with spiked heads most famously that of the Duke of York in 1460 during the Wars of the Roses. Queen Margaret in Shakespeare's *Henry VI* put the incident succinctly:

Off with his head, and set it on York gates
So York may overlook the town of York.

The last heads to be displayed here were those of Jacobites captured after the Battle of Culloden in 1745. Spectators on these walls in 1644 saw the disastrous aftermath of the Battle of Marston Moor when fugitives and wounded royalist survivors clamoured for admission with the Roundheads hot on their heels. Queen Elizabeth II and the Duke of Edinburgh were welcomed here by pageantry and fanfare when they formally sought entry to the city as part of the York's 1900th anniversary celebrations in 1971. A museum in the bar portrays the social history of York.

Micklegate heraldry

Micklegate was York's most important street – it led to the only bridge in the city over the River Ouse and was part of the long road between London and Edinburgh. Its importance attracted the richer residents of the city and medieval merchants, and leading Georgian businessmen built their town houses here.

Fine facade in Micklegate

Apart from business from passing traffic, Micklegate was close to the quays and the lucrative river trade. Look above today's shop fronts to see the character and quality of what were once fine town residences. In modern times the street has entered local folklore for the Micklegate Run, a pub crawl from the top of the hill to the bottom. **Micklegate House** ❹ is thought to have been built by John Carr for the Bourchier family and is probably the best of the town houses.

Opposite is **Holy Trinity Church** ❹. In medieval times the pageant wagons performing the religious Mystery Plays started their tour of the city from here. Inside the church is a memorial to Dr John Burton, a historian on

The Minster from the city walls

Jacob's Well and detail

St John Micklegate

View from Ouse Bridge

whom Laurence Sterne is said to have modelled Dr Slop in *Tristram Shandy*. Off Micklegate down Trinity Lane is **Jacob's Well 43**, a 15th-century timber-framed house with a canopied porch.

The hill down Micklegate towards the river was a severe test for horse-drawn traffic and until living memory had stone sets to give horses a better grip. **St Martin cum Gregory 44**, first mentioned in records in 1170, was enlarged in the 14th century but is no longer used for services. Roman masonry from a Temple of Mithras nearby can be seen in the tower plinth. The medieval Butter Market used to be held outside the church with produce being brought in from country areas for weighing and testing. William Peckitt, the glass painter (1731–95), is buried in the chancel.

Off on the left is George Hudson Street, formerly Railway Street and before that George Hudson Street – the original name being re-instated in 1971 when the city officially forgave Hudson for the disgrace he brought on York with his financial dealings. His rehabilitation continues with the council planning to commemorate his life with a monument.

St John Micklegate 45 is a mainly 14th- and 15th-century church saved from decay by finding a new use in modern times – first as the Institute of Advanced Architectural Studies and later as an arts centre. Now it is that unholiest of modern institutions – a gastropub.

Ouse Bridge was built between 1810 and 1821 and is the latest of at least three on the same site. The first had six arches and housed, along its entire length, public privies, a chapel, a toll booth and a prison. It appears early in the city's historical records because of a 'miraculous disaster'. So many people crowded on to it in 1154 to welcome Archbishop William into the city that it collapsed. No one died in the accident so it was hailed as a 'miracle' and William went on to become a saint.

Another stone bridge, just as crowded with buildings including a Council Chamber, had its two central arches and the houses above carried away in a flood in 1564. The repaired bridge still had houses on it up to the early 18th century. When there was need for further repairs the city tried unsuccessfully to raise money by petitioning the House of Commons for permission to dismantle the city walls and to use the stone and proceeds for bridge building. Work started on the present structure in 1810 and was not finished until 1820 – the old bridge being kept in use during the construction.

Looking downstream there is Kings Staith on the left and Queens Staith on the right – once the city's main dock area and still used by barge traffic supplemented by holiday craft. Corn and other bulky commodities came up river to this point to be unloaded by the 'common crane'. Queens Staith was the despatch centre for the butter trade coming from the butter market in Micklegate. In the 17th century some of the trade was not so savoury as barges parked here to carry away night-soil and dung. Regulations had to be imposed to ensure that cargoes were shifted as soon as they were loaded.

Retrace steps and on the upstream side of the bridge take a newly constructed elevated riverside walk past the Viking Hotel to ★ **All Saints, North Street** ⓪, which is famous for its stained glass and its 120ft (37m) spire, a striking landmark on the river frontage. Although there is Roman stonework in the structure and documentary references to All Saints in 1116, the main style of the church is 15th century when the spire was added. Softening the intrusion of the modern hotel across the road is a row of timber-framed cottages to its north side. (If the church is locked, the keys can be obtained from No. 1 All Saints Cottages.)

All Saints spire and interior

All Saints had a live-in anchoress in the 15th century with her own small doorway into the church. She was Dame Edith Rawghton, a wise woman who was said to be able to foretell the future and who was consulted by the king-maker Earl of Warwick. The tradition was revived early this century and an anchorite's cell in mock Tudor style was attached to the southwest corner of the church. A monk lived in what was reputedly the smallest house in Britain until some 20 years ago.

39

There was controversy in 1977 when the carvings in the church roof were restored in medieval colours, making the angels, according to some critics, look like glove puppets. The colours are now more subdued but there are complaints that the paintwork obscures the finer carving details. The church windows are from the 14th and 15th centuries. The east window of the chancel depicts John the Baptist, St Christopher, and St Ann showing the Virgin how to read. Other windows illustrate the Last Days of the World, legends taken from a version of *The Prick of Conscience*, a 14th-century poem telling of the world's end in earthquakes and fire. Another window shows the six *Corporal Works of Mercy* as set out in St Matthew and are said to be the only complete example of this subject in stained glass in England.

Painted angel

Among the angels in the glass in the south choir aisle is a medieval man wearing glasses – only two other examples of medieval spectacles appearing in stained glass are known, one in the southwest of England and the other in France.

A rare spectacle

Looking across the river, there is a view of the river frontage of the Guildhall (see Route 2, page 27).

Route 5

Steam trains, peacocks and picnics

National Railway Museum – Yorkshire Wheel – Museum Gardens – Yorkshire Museum – King's Manor – Theatre Royal *See map, pages 14–15*

This route starts at the National Railway Museum, crosses the river into the Museum Gardens with its peaceful Roman and medieval remains and takes in the King's Manor, the Theatre Royal and the Judge's Lodgings.

The Yorkshire Wheel

A steam giant

National Railway Museum

★★★ **The National Railway Museum** 🚂 (daily 10am–6pm, free) is probably the biggest and best railway museum in the world. The size of the place is impressive. The former York Motive Power Depot, covers nearly 2 acres (1 hectare) and has two huge turntables; it and the nearby Parcels Depot have both been superbly adapted for museum use. Exhibits still have direct access to the present-day railway system and occasionally go out on runs. A giant turntable inside the building is regularly activated. On display is a huge array of gleaming locomotives and rolling stock brought together by the combined collections of the former LNER Museum at York and the defunct British Transport Museum at Clapham in London. Engines can be climbed on, walked under and generally admired at close quarters. For those who want to see how they work an Ellerman Lines Pacific locomotive, rescued from a scrapyard in 1973 has been cut open to show its construction.

No such surgery was permitted on the collection's most famous locomotive, the shapely blue *Mallard*, which broke the world speed record for steam in 1938 by reaching 126mph (203kph). George Stephenson's tiny *Agenoria*, built in 1829, contrasts with the 190-ton steam monster, built in Britain in 1935 for China. Also on show is a history of Royalty's connection with trains and the style in which they liked to travel, including Queen Victoria's saloon which was said to be her favourite travelling 'home' for the journey to Balmoral from London. Trains used by the present Royal Family, until taken from service in 1977, are now drawn up at the platforms for everyone to see. 'Ordinary' passenger coaches range from the most primitive which ran on the Bodmin line in the 1830s to British Rail coaches from the 1950s.

Apart from the engines and the carriages the museum tells the full story of steam, diesel and electric rail travel and the inspiration it has provided for painters, photographers artists and craftsmen. Side galleries tell of the social and economic developments that followed in the

St Mary's Abbey

wake of steam with an audio-visual presentation in the museum theatre adding still more detail. Shunting noises and the 'click-clack' of trains going over the points drift from hidden loudspeakers to add to the nostalgia. It is difficult to get enthusiasts, however old, out of the place.

41

The museum is also the boarding point for the ★ **Yorkshire Wheel**, which opened in April 2006. Unlike the museum, there is a charge for this attraction. Another addition, expected in late 2007, is the opening of the museum's vast archives to the public in an expanded library.

Turn left out of the museum and take the road under the London-Scotland main railway line, before turning left again down a narrow lane and crossing the River Ouse by the footpath attached to the side of the Scarborough Railway Bridge. On the northern bank, walk towards the city passing the river defence walls with their waterproof gates designed to protect housing in the area after centuries of devastating flooding.

Turn into Marygate (where the floodgate is sunk into the road surface) and notice the medieval wall which starts at a riverside tower and runs to Marygate Tower in Bootham (*see Route 1, page 22*). These were the western defences of St Mary's Abbey. On the right is **St Olave's Church** ㊽, dedicated to the patron saint of Norway and founded by the Danish Earl Siward of Northumbria sometime before 1055. The prevailing style is 15th-century but during the siege of York in 1644 it was used as a gun platform and so badly damaged that it was largely rebuilt about 1721. The tomb of William Etty, the York artist, is in the churchyard.

St Olave's church: detail

Enter the ★★ **Museum Gardens** (summer 8am–8pm, winter until 5.30pm) by the path alongside the church through what remains of the main gate-house buildings of **St Mary's Abbey** ㊾. This botanical garden was laid out

Blooms in the gardens

in the early 19th century by the Yorkshire Philosophical Society in the grounds of what was once one of the most important abbeys in the north of England. All the trees and plants have been carefully selected and labelled, and peacocks and squirrels join visitors for picnics on the lawns. All that remains of the abbey church is a romantic ruined north aisle and part of the northwest pier from the crossing. The wall and its arches have been the backdrop for impressive revivals of the York Mystery Plays started in 1951 during which 'angels' appeared in the window arches and 'devils' romped in the nave.

After its foundation in 1080 the monks put a massive wall around their 12 acres (5 hectares) of land which lay just outside the city's defences but within the city precincts. As a result there were frequent arguments with York citizens over the abbey's rights. After the Dissolution of the Monasteries the abbey became an all too easy 'quarry' of ready dressed stone and it started to disappear. The masonry was carted off or taken away by boat to sites all over Yorkshire including Beverley Minster for repair work. The abbey's guest house or **Hospitium** 🟤 has been subjected to a modern restoration and is occasionally used for archaeological displays. Hidden by a copse of trees is a small **Astronomical Observatory** 🟤 (1831–33) which the Yorkshire Philosophical Society commissioned following the inaugural meeting of the British Association for the Advancement of Science in 1831. John Smeaton of Eddystone Lighthouse fame, designed the rotating roof. For a time its telescope was the largest of its kind in the world. The observatory was restored and re-opened by the Duke of Kent in 1981. The glare from modern city street lights now make observations difficult from this site.

Hospitium

42

Astronomical Observatory

The Yorkshire Museum

Resting the legs

Dominating the Gardens is the Greek-style, Doric column facade of the ★ **Yorkshire Museum** 🟤 (daily 10am–5pm, free). The region's most important archaeological, geological and natural history finds are stored here – thousands of specimens of minerals, rocks and fossils as well as the bones of prehistoric animals. The building was the creation of William Wilkins (designer of London's National Gallery) and it was completed in 1829 for the Yorkshire Philosophical Society. This group was established in 1823 as a result of the academic excitement prompted by the discovery of prehistoric remains in the Kirkdale Cave in North Yorkshire. The Crown leased the Society the ruins of the abbey and other land in the area to build their museum.

Galleries depict Roman, Anglo-Saxon and Viking life in the region. The Roman Gallery has a reconstruction of a Roman kitchen and displays of finds from 'digs' in York including the marble head of Constantine the Great who was proclaimed emperor in the city in AD306. Mosaics, tomb inscriptions, jewellery, coins and household utensils throw light on the domestic lives of the times. The Anglo-Saxon section has the silver gilt 8th-century Ormside Bowl and the beautifully decorated Gilling sword picked up by a boy while fishing in a stream in North Yorkshire. The Viking section displays leather goods and craftsmen's tools. In the basement the remains of the abbey, including the fireplace of the Warming Room, and life-size statues have been used *in situ* to re-create the atmosphere and tell the story of the vanished monastery. Other galleries are devoted to a fine collection of porcelain and to wildlife exhibitions. The museum has a programme of major exhibitions.

York's best example of the *Grandeur That Was Rome* lies to the right of the Museum. The **Multangular Tower** ㊾ marks the southwest corner of Roman York and gives some idea of the size of the walls and towers that surrounded the Roman city about AD300. The tower is Roman up to a height of 19ft (6m) where it becomes 13th-century, having been incorporated into the city's medieval defensive wall. For a view inside bear left of the tower to a path which leads up the embankment and through a doorway. Turn left and walk alongside the medieval wall to the 7th- and 8th-century ★ **Anglian Tower** ㊿, the site of a tragic archaeological dig. The tower had been buried within the ramparts for centuries but an exploratory trench cut into the earth mound in 1970 collapsed killing the archaeologist, Jeffrey Radley.

The earth mound supporting the medieval wall has been cut away to show the different heights of the city defences since Roman times.

Return through the hole in the wall and turn right along a lane and into Exhibition Square. Turn left into the entrance of the **King's Manor** ㊿. The Abbot of St Mary's used to live here until royalty took it over when the monasteries were disbanded. Henry VIII is thought to have stayed at King's Manor with Catherine Howard, James VI of Scotland visited on his way south to become James I of England, and Charles I stayed here twice when the Royal Court was in the city. His magnificent coat of arms are over the main entrance. In 1538 it then became the headquarters of the Council of the North and the residence of its Lord President. Once back in private hands it was divided into tenements, used as a girls' school, an assembly rooms for entertainments in the 18th century and then the home of the Yorkshire School for the Blind. Its present occupants are the University of York. Parts of the courtyard complex are open to the public including the Huntingdon Room in the north wing with its plaster friezes and fine chimneypiece.

The Multangular Tower

Layers of history at the Anglian Tower

43

Sign of royalty at the King's Manor

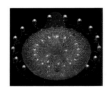

Theatre Royal

*The Minster from
Duncombe Place*

Turning right outside the King's Manor and across the road is the **De Grey Rooms** ❺❻, built in 1842 to house the officers' mess of the Yorkshire Huzzars during their annual visits to York; barristers also ate their meals here during the assizes. The Rooms took their name from Earl de Grey, Colonel of the Regiment, and were much used for concerts, balls and public entertainments. After World War II they were used for dances and now house the Tourist Information Offices.

The graceful sweep of tall terrace houses in **St Leonard's Place** was built in 1834 to provide 'genteel private residences'. To make the development possible the Corporation tore down some 350ft (100m) of the abbey walls to the south east of Bootham Bar. This has left the abbey's postern tower with a ragged wall edge stranded on the corner of the busy Bootham-Exhibition Square junction. St Leonard's takes its name from what was the largest medieval hospital in the north of England which was founded by William II. Before Henry VIII closed it down, the hospital dispensed food to the needy, cared for some 400 people, mostly retired Royal servants, and had a grammar school and 'bairn house' or orphanage. Charles I established a Royal Mint among its empty buildings and in 1782 some structures were pulled down so carriages could get better access to the new theatre. Still more buildings were destroyed in the construction of St Leonard's Place. The City Library occupies part of the land once taken up by the Royal Mint. Above ground the only remains of the medieval hospital are parts of an ambulatory and chapel near the City Library. The 'genteel residences' of St Leonard's have become council offices.

The history of the ★ **Theatre Royal** ❺❼ opposite starts in 1744 when the first theatre was built in the cloisters of St Leonard's Hospital. It was regarded as one of the

finest in the country outside London and catered for an acting company which made a circuit of local towns. In the 18th century its charismatic manager, Tate Wilkinson, raised the prestige of the theatre to something approaching that of the London stage.

He had to cope with unruly audiences and actors who considered his attempts at direction as an intrusion on their art. In his memoirs he records that the greatest profits came from the worst plays. The only time the 'classics' made a profit was when London stars like Sarah Siddons or John Philip Kemble came north to perform. It was Wilkinson's habit to watch new productions from the 'gods' (the seats at the top of the house) where he would hiss any bad acting. A section of the audience was once so incensed that they threw him out of his own theatre.

The theatre is still very much a thriving institution, despite a period of decline which lasted until the 1930s. The exterior is a Victorian form of Gothic with theatrical characters set in roundels while the inside retains all its intimate cosy atmosphere. A modern glass-fronted side extension built in 1967 provides a foyer, bars and restaurant area as well as much needed breathing space for theatre goers.

Thespian refreshments

45

Just around the corner in Duncombe Place is the imposing **Red House** ❺❽ with a torch snuffer at the door. Sir William Robinson, a Lord Mayor, built the house for himself, but in 1724 was put under pressure by the city to turn it into the official home for all the city's Lord Mayors. Sir William refused so the city built the Mansion House instead *(see page 26)*. The Red House is now utilised as an antiques centre. The name probably derives from the use of red brick instead of the city's more traditional stone.

Duncombe Place gives a fine view of the west front of York Minster but turning one's back on it go down Museum Street towards the river passing the **City Library** ❺❾ on the right and the only above-ground remains of **St Leonard's Hospital** ❻❶. At the entrance to the Museum Gardens turn left into Lendal.

The **Judge's Lodgings** ❻❶ (set back from the road) are where, from 1802 the Assize judges stayed having arrived with much pomp in the city to demand the sheriff to deliver up for judgment everyone held in the city jails. Dr Clifton Wintringham, a physician at the County Hospital, built the house in 1720 and the stone head above the door is that of Aesculapius, the God of Healing. With the re-arrangement of the court system after World War II the judges moved out and the building is now a hotel and restaurant.

Continue along Lendal to St Helen's Square, where this route ends, on the site of the Praetorian Gate, the main entrance to Roman York.

Red House: the torch snuffer

St Leonard's Hospital

Nearby flower arrangements

Route 6

Narrow streets

King's Square – Petergate – Minster Gates – Minster School – Minster Stoneyard – Goodramgate – Holy Trinity – Whip-ma-whop-ma-gate – DIG – Peasholme House – Black Swan – St Anthony's Hall – St Cuthbert's Church – Bar Walls – Merchant Taylors' Hall – Bedern Chapel *See map, pages 14–15*

Starting by flanking the Minster, this route circles the narrow streets in the city centre taking in shops, churches, a pub and a museum on the way.

Part of the summer scenery

Mad Alice Lane

46

Leave **King's Square** *(see Route 3, page 30)* and head up ★ **Low Petergate** towards the Minster's twin towers which can be seen above the distant roof tops. This is an attractive narrow street of shops with their overhanging upper storeys dating from Tudor and early Stuart times. Just beneath the road surface lies the wide, stone flagged, Via Principia of Roman York. On the right is the even narrower **Horn Pot Lane**, so called since the 13th century. An archaeological dig here in 1957–58 found the reason: a pit was discovered containing waste materials which showed that the local industry in the area had been making items out of horn.

To the left is, somewhat politically incorrect, **Mad Alice Lane**, one of York's many narrow snickleways. The lane is named after Alice Smith who was hanged in the 1830s and was reputedly insane. On the right is the Georgian frontage of what was York College for Girls; founded in 1907, it closed in 1997. Inside, older architectural features include a Tudor staircase.

Low Petergate

At **Minster Gates**  turn right to face the cathedral's south door and rose window. In the 13th century the Minster was surrounded by a 12ft (3.5m) wall and this was one of the four entrances into its precincts. Few traces of the wall remain. This section was demolished along with houses in Petergate when Duncombe Place was built in the 19th century.

Through Minster Gates turn right into Deangate. In 1903 it seemed a good idea to demolish property close to the cathedral and create a new road, but the Minster authorities came to regret it. Deangate became a major thoroughfare with heavy lorries shaking the cathedral's foundations. It was not until 1990 that the Minster authorities persuaded the City Council to stop the traffic and pedestrianise the area.

Tucked away on the right behind a small playing field is the **Minster School**  which was revived from ancient times in 1903 and installed in the building. Most of the children educated here are choristers in the cathedral. Before traffic was banned the students daily doffed their caps to waiting motorists as they processed over the pedestrian crossing into the cathedral for services. Next door is the **Minster Stoneyard**. If the gates are open, giant overhead saws can be seen cutting through blocks of stone as part of the continual repair work on the cathedral.

Waiting for treatment at the Minster Stoneyard

Turn right into Goodramgate where antique shops and boutiques occupy still more Tudor houses with half-timbered upper storeys. On the right is **Lady's Row**, a line of 11 tenements which contain elements of their 14th-century origins. Opposite them is a 20th-century development of pillarless concrete arches over shop fronts. It caused such an outcry in the 1960s that a strict watch was kept on all city centre 'improvements' thereafter.

Lady's Row

An iron gateway on the right gives entry to one of the prettiest, most secluded and almost forgotten churches in York, ★ ★ ★ **Holy Trinity, Goodramgate**  (Mon–Sat 10am–5pm, Sun 12–5pm). Stepping out of the busy street into a quiet churchyard one is faced with a venerable building with Jacobean box pews, uneven floors and an all-pervading atmosphere of antiquity. The church was built between 1250 and 1500 and has a two-tier pulpit (1785) and a reredos with the Ten Commandments, Creed and Lord's Prayer written out for worshippers. One can read the undulating floor for a history of York notables – in front of the communion rails is the stone which marks the resting place of the valet who attended Charles I. The side chapel has a 'squint' (a hole in the wall) so the priest at the chapel altar can see the high altar. The 15th-century tower has an unusual saddleback roof and 15th-century glass in the east window. Horn Pot Lane, already seen from Petergate, leads into a corner of the churchyard.

Holy Trinity interior

Salem Chapel

DIG

Peasholme House

The Black Swan

Keep right and back into Kings Square and down Colliergate, which becomes the shortest street in York – only some 35 yards (32m) long – but the one with the longest name: **Whip-ma-whop-ma-gate**. A plaque suggests the name is the local dialect of 1505 for: What a Street! Other explanations, however, persist. Nearby in Pavement is the site of the public whipping post and in medieval times the city also had an annual Whip Dog Day. A priest celebrating the mass once dropped a wafer and a dog ran off with it, so every St Luke's Day the custom was for schoolboys to remember the incident by whipping all dogs in the streets.

Down St Saviourgate on the left is the **Salem Chapel** ⓺⓯ with an Ionic portico and its entrance approached by a flight of steps. In its heyday in the 19th century it could accommodate nearly 1,700 people.

The inside of the redundant church of St Saviour opposite has been cleverly adapted to become **DIG** ⓺⓺ (daily 10am–5pm, admission charge) – another offshoot of the enterprising York Archaeological Trust who created the Jorvik Viking Centre *(see page 31)*. Here, budding young archaeologists can pick through trays of 'dig debris' sorting out bones and bits of pottery. The 'hands on' experience involves mapping the Viking dig site, examining human remains and reconstructing a unique Roman wall. High-tech videos help visitors explore and 're-build' ancient sites on the television screen.

Further down St Saviourgate there are Georgian town houses to the right and on the left the **Unitarian Chapel** ⓺⓻, the earliest of York's surviving nonconformist churches built 1692–93. Charles Wellbeloved, the eminent scholar and historian, was a minister here until 1858 and is buried here.

At the end of St Saviourgate turn right past **Peasholme House** ⓺⓼, a fine Georgian building dating from 1752 which was restored by the York Civic Trust in 1975 and turned into offices. Just inside the entrance to Aldwark on the left a plaque on the wall commemorates the use of this stark, plain building as the city's first **Methodist chapel** ⓺⓽. John Wesley preached at the opening service in 1759. Its religious use was discontinued in 1805 when larger premises were needed.

Across the busy Peasholme Green is the **Black Swan Public House** ⓻⓪, black-and-white timber-framed on the outside and with oak panelled rooms and open fires within. Sir Martin Bowes, goldsmith to Elizabeth I and Lord Mayor of London, had his family home here. Born in the house was the wife of General Wolfe who died in the assault on Quebec in 1759. The Black Swan was also a famous coaching inn and illegal cock-fighting took place on the first floor. A grill overlooks the stairs so someone could warn against the approach of the law.

The commercial buildings to the right of the public house cover what were the notorious Hungate slums. They were cleared before World War II and a new road, Stonebow, constructed. The name came from an ancient lane which could be a clue to York's greatest mystery: where is the Roman amphitheatre? The Viking derived name 'stonebow' could be a reference to amphitheatre ruins which the invaders may have found still standing when they took over the city.

St Anthony's Hall and detail

Turn left into Peasholme Green to **St Anthony's Hall** ㉛. The 15th-century guildhall of St Anthony has been taken over by York University and houses diocesan records as part of the Borthwick Institute of Historical Research. The outside of the building is a mixture of stone and brick while the main hall has a timbered ceiling with a number of fine carved rib joints or bosses. After the Dissolution of the Monasteries the corporation took over the guild and found a variety of uses for their new acquisition. It has been a workhouse, a prison, a knitting school for poor children, a military hospital during the Civil War and, in the early 18th century, the home of the Blue Coat School.

49

Next door **St Cuthbert's Church** ㉜ has an unusual success story. On the brink of being declared surplus to requirements in the 1970s the congregation suddenly blossomed and outgrew the 16th-century church and worshippers had to move into the much larger St Michael-le-Belfry near the Minster. A free standing glass 'bubble' was built inside St Cuthbert's to create offices and rooms for the St Michael's administration centre. The design won a prestigious architectural award in 1984.

St Cuthbert's

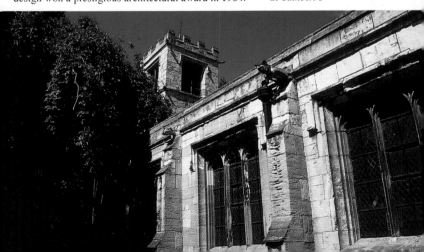

The Bar Walls

*Markings from the
City Wall Walk*

Oliver Sheldon House

Continue past St Cuthbert's and at the busy road junction over the River Foss climb up the steps onto the **Bar Walls** 🄰 *(see Route 1, page 21)*. The multi-storey car park seen from the walls covers the site of **Jewbury**, an area which the city's Jewish community acquired in Henry II's reign and which they later used as a cemetery. A plaque in English and Hebrew commemorates the site.

Inside the walls is **Aldwark** (meaning old fortifications), an area of neat new courtyards and town houses built since 1968 as part of a plan to bring people back to live in the centre of the city. The wall walk gives an aerial view of a residential success story. As one approaches Monk Bar *(see Route 1, page 21)* look down on a brick 'igloo' or **Ice House** 🄴 outside the walls. This is a structure built in 1800 to store ice for keeping larders cool. The ice was straw packed in a deep pit and the brick dome covered with soil.

Leaving the walls at Monk Bar, walk into the city and turn left into Aldwark to the ★ **Merchant Taylors' Hall** 🄵 (May–Oct Tues 10am–4pm, other times by appointment). Built in 1415, the building was for a long time in the hands of the Confraternity of St John, before being taken over by another powerful York guild formed in 1662 by the amalgamation of three groups of medieval craftsmen – the tailors, drapers and hosiers. It is the only example of a craft guildhall in the city and has a 60-ft (18-m) long Great Hall, with a 14th-century arch braced roof. The coat of arms at the end of the hall is that of the Stuarts, while that over the fireplace is of the Drapers of London. Drapers' coats of arms are also a feature of the Little Hall which has two heraldic windows. Guild members controlled the city's clothing trade but lost power when guild monopolies were removed in the early 19th century. The hall has since been used for a variety of social functions.

The Aldwark area, once filled with derelict warehouses, has been dramatically revived with town houses which can now be seen at close quarters. The restoration and conversion into residential accommodation of the Georgian fronted **Oliver Sheldon House** next door to the hall was part of the 'bring back the people' plan. The house is named after the founder and secretary of the York Civic Trust who died in 1951.

Turn right into St Andrewgate and right again into Bedern. On the left is **Bedern Chapel** 🄶, a building consecrated in 1347 as the chapel for the Vicars Choral of the Minster. *Bedern* is Anglo Saxon for house of prayer. The chapel is soon to become the workshop for galziers restoring the east windows of York Minster. The archway ahead leads into Goodramgate and back to the city centre.

Route 7

Merchant Adventurers' Hall

From riches to rags and a walk along the walls.

Pavement – Lady Peckitt's Yard – Merchant Adventurers' Hall – Fossgate – Walmgate – Walmgate Bar – Bar Walls to Fishergate Bar – Dick Turpin's Grave (optional continuation along the walls to Micklegate) *See map, pages 14–15*

This route starts in the richest area of medieval York, includes the city's finest guildhall, and continues through a former notorious slum area before taking to the bar walls for another semi-aerial view of the city.

Leave **Pavement** by a narrow lane alongside **Herbert House** *(see Route 3, page 31)* and into **Lady Peckitt's Yard**  for another glimpse of how the city must have looked in Tudor times. Black-and-white half-timbered buildings crowd together and at one point make a bridge over the lane. John Peckitt was Lord Mayor in 1702 and the yard's name comes from a local saying that while 'the mayor was a Lord for a year and a day, his wife is a Lady for ever and aye.'

Lady Peckitt's Yard

The lane emerges in Fossgate where the richest of the city's medieval merchants used to live. The furniture store opposite, however, is far from medieval. It has a startling terracotta tiled half-domed entrance decorated with swags of fruits in the Venetian style. It dates from 1911 when the premises were converted into the **Electric Cinema** .

Electric Cinema facade

Further down Fossgate on the right is a stone-framed doorway beneath the coat of arms of the York Merchant Adventurers – two winged horses supporting a shield and the motto: *Dieu Nous Donne Bonne Adventure*. The door leads to the magnificent ★★ **Merchant Adventurers'**

Fossbridge

52

Hall ⓐ (Apr–Sept Mon–Thur 9am–5pm, Fri and Sat until 3.30pm, Sun 12–4pm; Oct–Apr Mon–Sat 9am–3.30pm). This is the largest timber-framed building in the city and the home of the most powerful of the York guilds which closely guarded its trade with the outside world. The Great Hall has a massive timber-framed roof supported on braced beams and with Elizabethan panelling and uneven planked floor. Banners and portraits of past masters invoke the the hall's heyday.

The oldest section, the 14th-century stone undercroft is used for receptions and contains the Trinity Chapel with late-17th century seating and pulpit. Although starting life as a religious institution in 1357, the Guild soon went into business and played a leading role in the city's medieval prosperity. The Guild still holds meetings in its hall when its members wear robes and an 18th-century mace is carried before the Master. On leaving the hall, detour around to the grassed area in front for a better view of the half-timbered exterior.

Dorothy Wilson's Hospital

Back in Fossgate walk down to the arched and balustraded **Fossbridge** ⓑ built in 1811. The previous bridge was crowded with houses. Tenants were forbidden to put windows on the river side of their properties because they were used to dump rubbish into the river. The Foss retains its commercial uses. Barges loaded with newsprint pass under the bridge on their way to the local newspaper office in Walmgate on a completely waterborne journey from Scandinavia.

Over the bridge on the left, stone inscriptions on the house wall recall that this was the **Dorothy Wilson's Hospital** ⓒ which the good lady endowed in 1717 for the maintenance of 10 poor women and to teach 20 poor boys reading and writing. A monument in St Denys church up the road recounts her other charitable work.

Enter **Walmgate**, an area which is coming back to life after a grim and sordid past. Nineteenth-century records tell of a largely immigrant Irish population living here in wretched conditions, the women sitting on the kerb stones and smoking their pipes. As late as 1901 a 500-yard long stretch of road to Walmgate Bar boasted 20 public houses. Slum clearances have left gaps and the old properties that do survive look isolated among the new shops and businesses that are moving back. **St Denys Church** ⓲ on the right has windows of exceptionally fine mid-14th century glass. A vault belonging to the Percy family is thought to lie beneath the south aisle. One of the family, Henry, Earl of Northumberland, who was killed at the Battle of Towton in 1461, is believed to be buried here.

St Margaret's Church (83), largely rebuilt in 1851, has lost its medieval setting completely and is set back among trees with a backdrop of warehouses and council flats. Traces of the 17th-century building remain in the tracery of some windows but the doorway of the porch, 12th-century and heavily carved, is thought to have come from St Nicholas's Church in Lawrence Street. The restored church is now the National Centre for Early Music.

Again isolated by modernity across the street is **Bowes Morrell House** (84), a 14th-century timber-framed house which was restored and put into commercial use by the York Civic Trust in 1966.

Walmgate ends at ★ **Walmgate Bar** (85) – the most complete of the city's gateways and which has survived with its barbican intact. The portcullis hangs in its slot above the roadway and the 15th-century inner wooden door has its wicket gate still in place. The bar was badly battered by Parliamentarian cannon fire during the Civil War siege of the city and had to be extensively repaired. On the inner face of the gateway is an Elizabethan addition – a wood and plaster building with an ornamental palisade.

Steps can be retraced to the city centre from this point. The more energetic, or those in search of completion can finish the circuit of the city's bar walls with further optional breakaway points.

To the left the wall walk comes to a dead end after nearly a quarter of a mile at the brick-built **Red Tower**. The land between the tower and the re-start of the wall at Peasholme Green was marshy and regarded as militarily impassable. William the Conqueror damned the River Foss to get water into his castle ditches and the flooded area became a valuable royal fishpond.

To the right from Walmgate Bar the parapet walk runs for just over a quarter of a mile to Fishergate Bar, passing on the way the city's **Barbican Entertainments Cen-**

Walmgate

St Denys Church stained glass

Walmgate Bar

Barbican Entertainments Centre

Dick Turpin's Grave

tre and swimming pool which were constructed on what was the city's cattle market. Descend at Fishergate Bar. Turn right into George Street and in St George's Churchyard, across the road from the actual church, is **Dick Turpin's Grave** ❸❻. A modern tombstone replaces the original worn away stone. After being hung for highway robbery in 1735, Turpin was buried here twice. The first time the corpse was stolen but was subsequently retrieved by a mob and reburied.

Head toward Fishergate Tower and cross the Foss at Castle Mills Bridge. To the left beyond the locks are the modern flood barriers which control the flow of the Foss into the Ouse. The route can end here by returning to the city centre via Clifford Street. Alternatively, cross the River Ouse via **Skeldergate Bridge** ❸❼ and complete the circuit of the city walls. Until 1875, when the bridge was built, a ferry took people across the river at this point. Downstream on the nearside bank is St George's Field where hangings took place and the ducking stool was operated. Standing on the bridge looking upstream at the far bank the old warehouses fronting the river have been converted into either restaurants or offices. Downstream a modern development has created flats and penthouses with a riverside view.

54

The Bar Walls begin again immediately across the bridge at **Baile Hill** ❸❽, a large mound once topped by another of William the Conqueror's wooden and moated castles. The hill was planted with trees in the early 18th century and a century later a prison was built here only to be demolished in 1880 and the stone used for the foundations of the nearby bridge.

Baile Hill

A pleasant half-mile walk along the ramparts with distant views of the Minster over the chimney pots ends at

Skeldergate Bridge

Micklegate Bar *(see Route 4, page 36).*

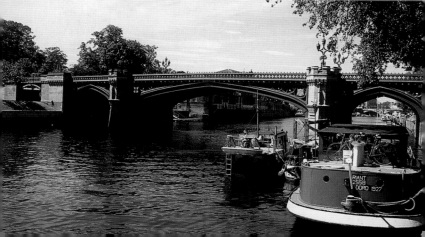

Excursions

Stately homes, castles, abbeys and pretty villages all lie within easy reach of York as well as the North York Moors National Park and a coast line with a choice of cheerful holiday resorts. The area has a framework of good roads before one has to take to the country lanes. The attractions are varied and scattered but all those listed below are within 50 miles (80km) of York and can be easily reached and explored in a day by car. Using the map (*see page 56*), a number of places of interest can be combined into excursions according to taste. The mileages shown against each entry are from York and some sights can be located on the map by a reference number.

North York Moors idyll

North York Moors

The ★★ **Moors** start north of Pickering and encompass the largest expanse of heather in England and Wales broken by streams and valleys and pockets of green fields. After the agricultural order of the Vale of York they create an atmosphere of wild openness and freedom. There are spectacular views from the A169 over the **Hole of Horcum**, a great amphitheatre thought to have been scooped out of the moors at the end of the ice age. The moorland villages of **Goathland** and **Grosmont** are worth a visit. There are areas of afforestation such as **Dalby Forest**, which has a popular 9-mile (14-km) drive which brings visitors close to wild deer and bird life. There are several places along the drive to stop for fishing or picnics. The park also runs a network of buses to ease congestion in the park. Day tickets on the Moorsbus network begin at £3 (tel: 01845 597000). Go to www.visitthemoors.co.uk for more information. (45–50 miles/70–80km)

55

Lively Scarborough

The coast

A day out at the seaside is part of Yorkshire folklore. Bustling, lively **Scarborough**, northeast of York, calls itself the Queen of Watering Places, offering visitors two bays, a busy harbour and a castle on the cliff top. The South Bay has a typically brash English seaside front but the areas around the Spa and the North Bay have a pleasantly contrasting calm. Behind the seafront and up the hill is a modern shopping centre and an abundance of cafés and entertainments. The town has an enviable theatrical reputation built around Alan Ayckbourn, the local-born playwright. (40 miles/65km)

    Whitby, further north, is an old whaling port, the town and harbour picturesquely cramped between the sides of a steep river valley. The ruined Abbey of St Hilda (AD657), looks down on the town and is reached by 199 'church steps'. Whitby was home to Captain Cook and the house

Picturesque Whitby

in Grape Lane where he lodged as an apprentice has been turned into a memorial museum. (50 miles/80km)

Robin Hood's Bay, just south of Whitby, nestles picturesquely at the foot of a steep cliff road. The village has lost scores of its houses to the sea over the last two centuries – but it is still there. This smugglers' haunt now attracts fossil hunters. (45 miles/70km)

Bridlington, east of York, has fine sandy beaches on either side of the harbour with the town and front very much given over to the holidaymaker. (40 miles/65km)

Filey, north of Bridlington, is a quieter holiday town with gardens and good beaches. Nearby Flamborough Head is popular with birdwatchers. (40 miles/65km)

Nearby towns

Harrogate, west of York, is a spa town famous for its flowers, parks and Georgian and Victorian terraces. The Royal Pump Room on Royal Parade is now a museum, and the sulphurous and chalybeate waters continue to bubble. The town offers Turkish baths, sauna and solarium – and high-quality shopping. (20 miles/30km)

Once tightly enclosed by medieval walls, **Beverley**, east of York, has long since burst its defences and only the imposing 15th-century North Bar or gateway remains. The former capital of the East Riding of Yorkshire, is an important market town with many 18th- and 19th-century houses and shop fronts. The Gothic Minster with two bell towers, rich in stone and wood carvings, is a landmark visible for miles across the flat landscape. (30 miles/50km)

★ **Helmsley**, north of York, is an attractive country town with a Friday market, handsome houses and good quality shops all of which have made it a popular 'day-out' for summer motorists. William Wordsworth and his sister are

Life on the water

Browsing in Helmsley

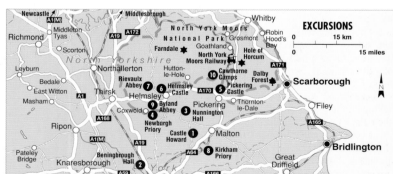

EXCURSIONS

said to have stayed at the half-timbered Black Swan and for thousands of visitors it is the place to take afternoon tea. Behind Helmsley Castle *(see page 58)* is a walled garden with heritage apples and Victorian greenhouses. Nearby are Duncombe Park *(see page 58)* and Rievaulx Abbey. (30 miles/50km)

★ **Pickering** is another charming and ancient market town with a number of tourist attractions. Apart from the castle ruins *(see page 58)*, it is the starting point for the privately run North York Moors Railway. Steam and diesel trains come right into the centre of town and take passengers on an 18-mile (30-km), hour long, scenic trip over the moors to Grosmont (www.northyorkshiremoorsrailway.com). Pickering's parish church is reason enough to visit; it has some of England's finest 15th-century wall paintings and a Georgian house by the river holds the Beck Isle Museum of Rural Life (Apr–Oct daily 10am–5pm, admission charge), which has exhibits on old printing presses, cobbler and hardware shops. (30 miles/50km)

Malton, northeast of York, is a busy market town serving an important agricultural region. Its museum displays local archaeological finds and there are two nearby diversions. **Eden Camp** (www.edencamp.com) recalls modern military history and **Flamingo Land** is a zoo with roller coasters and thrill rides (www.flamingoland.co.uk). (18 miles/ 30km)

Stately homes

★★★ **Castle Howard** ❶, one of the most popular excursions from York (house Mar–Oct daily 11am–6.30pm; shops daily 10am–5pm), stands on a hilltop overlooking a landscaped lake and is forever associated with the TV production of *Brideshead Revisited*. Designed by Sir John Vanburgh, this is country living on the grand scale – a marbled, domed entrance hall, staterooms lavishly furnished with Sheraton and Chippendale and on the walls Old Masters such as Rubens and Canaletto. The 1,000-acre (400-hectare) grounds are laid out with fountains, gardens, a playground and ornamental structures such as the Temple of the Four Winds. The Stable Courtyard at the entrance has been renovated and now houses a café, a farm shop selling local food and ales, a bookshop and a chocolate shop. Entrance to this area is free. (15 miles/25km)

Owned by the National Trust, **Beningbrough Hall** ❷ (Mar–June, Sept and Oct Sat–Wed; house: noon–5pm, grounds 11am–5.30pm; admission charge) is a fine 18th-century house set in a 375-acre (150-hectare) wooded park with formal gardens in which you can picnic. Inside there is a grand staircase, fine decorative woodcarvings and an exhibition of 17th- and 18th- century portraits. Children will enjoy the nature trail and playground. (8 miles/13km)

The road to Castle Howard

57

Castle Howard

Beningbrough Hall

Nunnington Hall

Pickering Castle

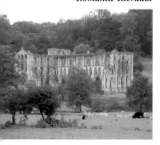

Romantic Rievaulx

Kirkham Priory

Also National Trust-owned, **Nunnington Hall** ❸ (Mar–Nov Wed–Sun 1.30–5pm; Tues also in June, July and Aug; admission charge) is a 16th- and 17th-century riverside manor house which looks as if the Cavaliers and Roundheads have only just moved out. Tea is served in formal walled gardens. Inside are fine tapestries and china and upstairs the Carlisle Collection of Miniature Rooms showing different styles of decor and furniture and a series of craft workshops with miniature tools. (20 miles/30km)

Newburgh Priory ❹ (Apr–June Sun and Wed, house: 2.30–4.45pm, gardens: 2–6pm; admission charge) is an 18th-century house with fine water gardens. The family had links with Oliver Cromwell and part of his remains are said to be here in a sealed tomb. There are also good views of the Kilburn White Horse in the distance. (20 miles/30km)

Duncombe Park near Helmsley is the 'poor' man's Castle Howard, with many miles of parkland to explore and elegant period rooms to see. (30 miles/50km)

Fountains Abbey, north of Harrogate is another atmospheric set of monastic ruins. It also has a deer park filled with red, fallow and sika deer. (25 miles/40km)

Castles, abbeys and camps

Originally a royal hunting lodge, **Pickering Castle** ❺ (Apr–Sept daily 10am–6pm, Oct Thur–Mon 10am–4pm; admission charge) is now an ideal sheltered place for family outings and picnics. The circle of walls is complete and the central motte or mound gives superb views over what, in medieval times, were forests filled with highly prized deer. (25 miles/40km)

Helmsley Castle ❻ (Apr–Sept daily 10am–6pm, Oct Thur–Mon 10am–5pm, Nov–Mar Thur–Mon 10am–4pm) is a well-preserved Tudor Hall and ruined keep that dominates the market town. In nearby Duncombe Park, Lord Feversham has restored the mansion for family use. There are parklands and riverside walks. (28 miles/45km)

Situated in a steep sided, peaceful valley, the romantic ruins of ★ **Rievaulx Abbey** ❼ (Apr–Sep daily 10am–6pm, Oct Thur–Sun 10am–5pm, Nov–Mar Thur–Mon 10am–4pm; admission charge) are the former home of a 13th-century community of monks. (35 miles/55km)

Kirkham Priory ❽ (Apr–Aug daily 10am–6pm, Sep until 4pm, Oct Sat and Sun only) is another picturesque ruin, this time on the banks of the River Derwent. Founded in 1125, it was greatly enlarged in the following two centuries before losing its community at the Dissolution and relapsing into peaceful, rural obscurity. (12 miles/20km)

Byland Abbey ❾ (Apr–Oct 10am–6pm) was the home of a Cistercian community but only part of the west front of the Abbey remains. Floor tiles show the lines of the rest of the church and monastic buildings. Remains of an ancient hostelry were found under the Abbey Inn in 2006, linking the pub with its predecessor. (20 miles/32km)

Cawthorne Camps  is where Roman soldiers stationed in York were taken for their summer training exercises. They camped out here and practised ditch digging and rampart erecting. Not a great deal to see but an invigorating and intellectually rewarding walk among the banks and hollows. (35 miles/55km)

And pretty villages...

Hutton-le-Hole on the edge of the moors probably takes the 'picture post-card' prize with its weavers' cottages set well back from the beck that dissects a rolling, sheep cropped village green. The reconstructed agricultural buildings of the Ryedale Museum shows rural life before tourists. **Thornton-le-Dale** is another contender with a stream running down the village street and pretty cottages fronted by flowers. **Farndale** is famous for its 2-mile (3-km) daffodil walk along the River Dove. Set within the National Park **Coxwold** has a long street of stone cottages set back from the road and fronted with broad grass verges. Laurence Sterne, author of *Tristram Shandy*, was the village clergyman here and his house, Shandy Hall, with its crooked chimney, has been renovated by the Sterne Trust.

Ryedale Museum at Hutton-le-Hole

59

Outskirts of York

Yorkshire Air Museum (daily 10am–5pm, closes 3.30pm in winter, admission charge) is located in a World War II flying control tower on the airfield at Elvington, restored in memory of allied air crews who flew from airfields around York. (8 miles/12km)

Sutton Park is a charming, early Georgian lived-in house overlooking award-winning gardens that has a tearoom for visitors to relax in. (8 miles/12km)

Thornton-le-Dale

Architectural Heritage

Romans to Vikings

Roman legionnaires founded York in AD71 while on a conquering raid into Northern Britain. The 50-acre (20-hectare) fortress soon had massive limestone walls, gateways and watch towers and famous Roman Emperors like Constantine, Severus and Hadrian came and went with their armies. Two modern streets, Petergate and Stonegate, follow the Roman street pattern and some 10ft (3m) below the modern city the rest of Eboracum still lies buried with its barrack blocks, houses and bath buildings.

At the heart of the Roman city was the colonnaded forum of the legionary headquarters, now buried deep beneath the cathedral. From here Roman authority held sway over northern Britain and at times over the whole Roman world when Emperors were in residence. Today the only above ground evidence of what Roman York must have looked like is the Multangular Tower in the Museum gardens. But over the years countless excavations have uncovered statues, gravestones and other relics which testify to the power and status of the city.

Historians still debate what happened to Roman York after the legions left. The Saxons had a trading post on the river bank (confirmed by excavations when a new hotel was built in Fishergate) and then the Vikings sailed up the Ouse, raped, pillaged and settled outside the walls of the decaying city. The wooden walls of Viking homes were found in excavations in Coppergate. They have been 're-buried' under a new shopping precinct but can still be reached and seen in the Jorvik Viking Centre. It was the Vikings not the Romans who gave York its modern name – York being a corruption of Jorvik.

Gothic

Medieval times, despite plagues and civil wars, saw York grow and thrive as a trading city dominated by the powerful craft guilds. Its merchant adventurers used their magnificent guildhalls for business and entertainment. They provided the wealth not only to encircle their city with defensive walls, but also the faith to start work on building a huge new cathedral. Generations of craftsmen, fathers and sons, were involved in its construction many of them knowing that they would never see its completion. The Minster took some 250 years in the making, its Gothic style changing subtly over the years. As a result, unlike many other cathedrals it cannot be given a precise architectural label. The great Nave is in the Decorated Style; the choir and eastern section is Perpendicular and the North and South Transepts, Early English. Yet all the different styles fuse into one glorious aesthetic whole.

Opposite: Constantine outside the Minster

The Roman Column

61

The Anglian Tower

Chapter House vaulting

Stained glass

Glass at All Saints, North Street

As the masons worked and the Minster slowly took its present form, artistry of a different kind was flourishing in small studios all over the city. York was becoming a major centre for glass painting. The whole history of English stained glass, ranging from the 12th century to the present day, can be seen within the cathedral. And the medieval artists were not overawed by their subject matter – there was always a place for humour despite the seriousness of the Biblical stories they were illustrating. The professions are 'aped' in one Minster window with a monkey doctor tossing a urine bottle in the air; in the West Window a nativity scene has a smiling cow.

Bellfounder's window, the Minster

Most of the glass survived not only the Reformation and the clumsy repair work of the plumbers and glaziers of that period but also the Civil War of 1642–49. The city was put under siege by Roundheads who did not care for the 'idolatrous imagery' of stained glass. The city, however, was fortunate that it was a fellow Yorkshireman, Sir Ferdinando Fairfax, who was in charge of those trying to batter their way in. He put the cathedral and all of York's churches under his protection saving a glowing tradition of stained glass for later generations to enjoy.

62

Tudor to the present

Tudor times saw local craftsmen building half-timbered houses with overhanging upper storeys. Most were simple artisans' homes but others, such as the heavily carved Herbert House in Pavement, were grand and ornate representing the wealth and status of the city merchants. The purest examples of their skills can be seen in the heavy timbering of the Merchant Adventurers' Hall and the admittedly much restored shops in the Shambles.

Merchant Adventurers' Hall

Another era brought in another style – Georgian, with its ordered neatness and symmetry putting red brick alongside half timbering in many York streets. John Carr, who began life as a workman builder and later became Lord Mayor of his native city, designed the first grandstand on Knavesmire as well as the Assize Courts and the County Hospital in Monkgate. Georgian homes, such as the Mansion House and Fairfax House, reflected the prosperity of at least some of the population and show the lifestyles of those who took part in the great social flowering of York.

The Victorians added their architectural style: a very grand Station Hotel to compliment their 'cathedral to steam' – the new railway station – as well as the new Law Courts in Clifford Street.

Although neo-Georgian style housing has been accepted in the revitalisation of the Aldwark area, post-war insertions of 'modern' architecture into the city's streetscape aroused fierce controversy in Goodramgate and Stonebow.

Society and the Arts

Street theatre

Mystery plays

Jugglers and tumblers at the great medieval fairs provided locals with their first taste of 'theatre' and their successors, the buskers, are still around today tossing flaming torches in the air and teetering about on monocycles.

But it was a monk working quietly in his cell at St Mary's Abbey who is thought to have been responsible for putting depth and power into the city's street theatre. He produced the York Cycle of Mystery Plays – with its plot spanning the Creation to the Day of Judgment. With powerful simplicity and earthy humour the Plays present a stark choice between Good and Evil – Heaven and its Angels and Hell with its romping, pitch-fork wielding devils. The amateur actors of the city's guilds performed the plays with pageant wagons as mobile stages. And once a year the procession of wagons would set off from Holy Trinity in Micklegate, each guild performing its play at different stations around the city. York had a holiday and a religious experience all at the same time, but the Plays ran into trouble with the Reformation. Disputes arose about some of its theology and in the streets the holiday spirit occasionally got out of hand. Religious leaders complained of drunken irreverence and in 1572 they called in all the play books 'for examination' – and kept them. The Plays were not publicly performed again for nearly 400 years.

The 1996
York
Cycle
of
Mystery
Plays
4 - 30
June

YORK

BOX OFFICE
☎ 01904 623568
24 HOUR INFO LINE
☎ 01904 610041

63

An ancient tradition revived

Balls, assemblies and hangings

Horse racing and the assizes propelled the city's culture and its 'entertainments' into a new glittering age during the early part of the 18th century. Horse racing had been held in the city since 1530 but in 1731 the City Council, shrewdly realising the commercial possibilities, moved them onto Knavesmire and improved the facilities with an

Grand Opera House

Theatre Royal detail

A variety of street music

eye to attracting the nobility. Races have been held there ever since. They were quickly patronised by Royalty and the local aristocracy and a regular 'season' developed. The nobility and gentry soon needed somewhere fitting to meet socially. The answer was the Assembly Rooms – an Egyptian-style hall glittering with chandeliers in which society could dance, play cards or just walk, talk and be seen. Royal dukes were frequent visitors and the city quickly became the North's social and fashion centre.

The other York 'season' followed the arrival of the Assize judges with their Royal Orders for the City Fathers to open all the jails and hand over all the prisoners for judgment. Jacobites from Bonnie Prince Charlie's 1745 rebellion were tried here as well as the Luddites and Dick Turpin. Of more interest to the crowds was the fact that the convicted were also publicly hanged – the prisoners being paraded through the city to the gallows on Knavesmire with vendors selling ballads about their deeds. A new 'drop' on St George's Field, closer to the jail, shortened the journey but did not dim the interest in the spectacle. Even in the early 19th century there were complaints that the railway company was not putting on enough excursions to convey outsiders to the more popular hangings.

On an intellectual level the coffee houses flourished providing literary inspiration for Laurence Sterne who loved these 'chit chat' clubs and is said to have used the people he met there as characters in his writings. Dr John Burton, well known as a local Jacobite and Tory, was lampooned as Dr Slop – Sterne being of the Whig persuasion.

Theatre

In the theatre's early days attempts at imparting culture followed the 'seasons.' The Theatre Royal was built to entertain the noble and not so noble who crowded into the city for the races, the assizes, or just to attend the markets. The most charismatic of the theatre managers, Tate Wilkinson, soon discovered that the classics did not pay the bills. It was only the coarser entertainments, he said, that made a profit and the only way he could make money out of Shakespeare was through the 'star' system. People would turn up to watch if Sarah Siddons or John Philip Kemble were performing. But he persisted – staging not only Shakespeare but works by 18th-century playwrights soon after the London openings of their plays. He even staged opera and oratorio and succeeded in giving York a prestige approaching that of the London theatres.

For those who could not afford the theatre, there were travelling showmen and the City Waits (York's official musicians) playing for processions and on all public occasions. For a time the city revelled in being at the heart of the North's cultural and social life.

Decline and revival

York's Lord Mayor, George Hudson, with his obsession to 'mak' all t'railways cum to York', did the social life of his city a grave disservice. It had taken up to four days to make the journey to London by coach and this had localised the activities of northern society. But now the railway advertisements promised: 'Breakfast in York and tea in the capital.' The passion for balls faded and the attractions of the capital proved too compelling. York's grand social scene drifted away on a cloud of hissing steam.

In 1835 the stage of the Theatre Royal was so decayed that it was dangerous for the actors.

The Festival of Britain in 1951 saw York reviving the Mystery Plays. In keeping with tradition, scores of local people took part as amateur actors or in making the costumes. Instead of pageant wagons there was an open-air stage production with the ruins of St Mary's Abbey as a backcloth. It was a huge popular and artistic success and became the centre piece for a series of triannual Festivals of the Arts at York. Around the Plays were gathered orchestral concerts, art exhibitions, and other drama.

But as with their earliest productions the Plays have attaracted controversy – the latest being the casting of a woman to play God. Nevertheless, York's scene is thriving again especially during summer's peak tourist season when the majority of the city's 4 million visitors pass through the city. The Theatre Royal is as popular as ever and the Grand Opera House has reopened after a long, bleak spell as a bingo hall, while the city's modern Barbican Centre has become the venue for visiting shows and popular entertainers.

York also draws on its bountiful surroundings and history for several popular annual festivals including the Jorvik Viking Festival in February, the Early Music Festival in December and the Food and Drink Festival in September.

Mystery Play in medieval times

The band plays on

A moment of reflection

Food and Drink

Opposite: a quiet night in the Shambles

York's claim to culinary fame rests almost entirely on York Ham and Yorkshire Puddings. York Ham refers to a type of curing that involves salt and light smoking. Folklore suggests the name came about because oak shavings from the building of the Minster were used for smoking.

Yorkshire Puddings are making a come-back, thanks perhaps to the new frozen varieties, which ensure that they rise perfectly every time. Most cafés and pubs in and around the city have them on their menus, usually served with traditional onion gravy. The original Yorkshire promise to guests was that the more pudding you ate the more meat you got – if you had any appetite left to eat it. To 'careful' Yorkshire folk, puddings were cheap and meat was expensive.

Many country cafés still serve Yorkshire High Teas, substantial affairs involving fried ham, eggs and sausages followed by apple pie and cheese. Even ordinary teas are generous, often involving spiced tea cakes and 'fat rascals', scone-like buns full of dried fruit and cherries.

An elegant lunch in York can be savoured at **Betty's** in St Helen's Square, but office workers and many visitors are happy with just a snack, which means choosing between a bewildering selection of city centre pubs offering sandwiches, shepherd's pies and the usual chips-with-everything fare. Now there is also a host of upmarket coffee bars. One can lunch *al fresco* on the riverbank outside the **Kings Arms** at King's Staith; inside the crowded, atmospheric **Star Inn** in Stonegate or in the Elizabethan timbered rooms of the **Black Swan** in Peasholme Green.

Visitors with cars might choose to drive out into the countryside around York, which can be particularly pleasant in the evening. There they will find a host of attractive village pubs offering good, wholesome, home-cooked food in a tranquil setting. The secret is to consult local people – they all have their own favourite country eating place to recommend.

Some York institutions

67

Restaurant selection

The following restaurants, either in or within easy reach of the city, are listed according to three categories:
£££ = expensive (over £50 for two)
££ = moderate (£30–50 for two)
£ = inexpensive (under £30 for two)

Betty's Tea Room, St Helen's Square, tel: 01904 659142. 1930s decor and sophisticated atmosphere. Lunches and snack meals available as well as the famous afternoon teas complete with sumptuous cake trolleys. **£**
Blake Head, 104 Micklegate, tel: 01904 623767. A vegetarian café with modest prices and devoted clientele. **£**

The Black Swan

Blue Bicycle, Fossgate, tel: 01904 673990. Lively restaurant with a great atmosphere and reputable food. **£££**

The Grange, Clifton, tel: 01904 644744. The Ivy Restaurant in this hotel has an established reputation for first-class food. **£££**. There is a broad brasserie menu in the brick-vaulted cellars. **£**

Jaipur Spice, Haxby Road, tel: 01904 673550. Excellent Indian cooking. **££**

Kites, Grape Lane, tel: 01904 641750. A sparse decor of bare floors and white painted brick, but the food is excellent. Standard dishes are done well and there is an imaginative menu plus a new wine bar downstairs. **£**

Little Betty's, Stonegate, tel: 01904 622865. Pass through a downstairs shop that resonates with the smell of coffee beans and enter the small rooms upstairs for similar fare to that offered at Betty's further down the street. **£**

Maxi's Restaurant, Ings Lane, Nether Poppleton, tel: 01904 783898. Highly rated Chinese cuisine. **£**

Melton's, Scarcroft Road, tel: 01904 634341. A restaurant of high quality. The owners learned their cooking with the Roux brothers and the continental and oriental influences can be seen in the varied and imaginative menu. **£££**

Le Meridien York, Station Road, tel: 01904 653681. Former grand railway hotel where the traditional restaurant elegance still lingers. **££**

Middlethorpe Hall, Bishopthorpe Road, tel: 01904 641241. A little way out of town but elegant dining in country-house style. **£££**

Mulberry Hall, Stonegate, tel: 01904 620736. Up above the porcelain shop for light lunches and teas served in civilised surroundings. **£**

Park Inn York, North Street, tel: 01904 459988. Choice of either the brasserie or à la carte menu. Good views over the river while you dine. **£££**

Ristorante Bari, Shambles, tel: 01904 633807. Lively Italian atmosphere with a full Italian menu (not just pizzas and pasta) served with Mediterranean panache. **£**

St William's College Restaurant, College Street, tel: 01904 634830. Just around the corner from the Minster and tastefully fitted into a corner of the half-timbered courtyard. Good quality snacks with an overspill area into the courtyard during the summer. **£**

Tricksters Lane, Fossgate, tel: 01904 675576. Continental-style food of high quality, with fish a speciality. **£££**

Shopping

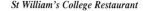

York has always been a market centre catering for the needs of a largely rural hinterland but tourism has put gilt on the gingerbread. The variety and quality of shops is remarkable. **Coney Street** is still regarded as the main

The Royal York

St William's College Restaurant

Picnic in style

Cooling off

shopping thoroughfare but it is little different from any other busy high street in England. The great multiples and chain stores overshadow the small boutiques and shoe shops. Other shopping areas, however, have sprung up.

New shopping

York's newest street, **Coppergate Walk**, has been a run-away commercial success and has pulled the city's traditional shopping patterns eastwards. Built over the Coppergate excavations, the Walk is narrow and has an almost medieval cosiness and scale despite its modernity. Here are Body Shop, Dorothy Perkins, Evans, Clarks and Dolcis, all crowded together before the street opens out into a lively square where larger stores such as Fenwick, Marks & Spencer and Prestons the Jewellers dominate the scene. Food and sport outlets are interspersed among the clothes shops and the presence of the queues for the Jorvik Viking Centre ensure a lively, cosmopolitan atmosphere.

Old city shopping

The distinctive olde-worlde shopping scene has shifted from Coney Street – it is now **Stonegate** that lays claim to shopping with style. Mulberry Hall displays its fine porcelain in the downstairs windows of the medieval, half-timbered bishop's house. Quality jewellers, such as Inglis and Son and Barbara Cattle, fit snugly into the other old houses in the street along with art shops, bookshops, the Stonegate Teddy Bear Shop and boutiques such as Droopy and Brown's.

In **Petergate** there are more boutiques, such as Giselle, as well as Culpeper the Herbalist. Leading off Petergate on the right is the **Swinegate** area of the city, once run-down and desolate, now rebuilt in neo-Georgian style and slowly attracting new shops and customers.

The **Shambles**, the city's most visited street, is no longer the home of the butchers, and has been taken over by the

Stylish shopping in Stonegate

tourist trade – gift, craft shops, leather and knitwear. There is also Pickerings, said to be the city's oldest bookshop, a tea room and a pizza parlour. Nearby is **Fossgate** which is coming back to commercial life with furniture stores, book and antique shops. Running parallel to Coney Street is **Davygate**, home to stylish shops such as Laura Ashley, Accessorize, Austin Reed, Gap and Debenhams. And on the corner of St Sampsons Square there is the city's own home-grown department store, WP Brown's. **Parliament Street**, with plane trees and a fountain, has become the city's central piazza. The Disney Store has moved in to join Accessorize and an enlarged Marks and Spencer. Facing each other across the street is Pret à Manger and the Thornton's Toffee Cabin. **High Ousegate** has a Waterstone's bookshop and Habitat. **Lendal**, just off St Helen's Square, has Banks the music shop and the York Antique Centre is at No 2.

The Shambles

A short walk up High Petergate and through Bootham Bar brings one to **Gillygate**, which has acquired a distinctive range of shops. For years the street was threatened with demolition and was 'planning blighted'. When the threat was lifted, a number of traders, many of whom had been forced out of the city centre by high rents, moved into the neighbourhood. The result has been a delightful mix of small antique shops, bric-a-brac and various arts and crafts establishments.

Parliament Street in high season

Although the open-air markets, for which the city has been famous for centuries, continue to flourish, these days they tend to be smaller than their illustrious predecessors. Nevertheless, everything from foodstuffs (especially fish and fruit) to clothing and crockery is on offer every weekday in **Newgate**, which is situated to the rear of The Shambles.

Where the haunting begins

The area just north of York abounds with traditional cabinet and fine furniture makers. Design in Wood in Thirsk (tel: 01845 525010) leads the way but other quality shops include Coxwold Cabinet Makers (tel: 01347 868530), Old Mill Furniture (tel: 01845 597227) and Fox Furniture (tel: 01845 501359). Craftsmen of a different sort operate at Cropton Brewery near Pickering. Their fine ales are widely available in York (www.croptonbrewery.co.uk).

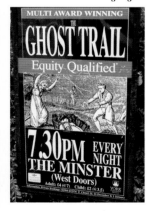

Further Activities

The Races

Racing has a long history in York and it still plays a significant role in the city's sporting and social calendar. Every year there are 15 meetings at one of England's most attractive courses with its superb new stands on Knavesmire (www.yorkracecourse.co.uk). The three-day August meeting, the Ebor Festival, is the biggest event of the year –

International Day on the Tuesday, the Ebor Handicap on the Wednesday and Ladies Day on Thursday when fashion is on parade. According to the locals: 'We are not the Ascot of the North – Ascot is the York of the South'.

Dressed for the races

River trips

Races of a different kind can be seen on the River Ouse during the annual Jorvik Viking Festival in February. Boat crews from Scandinavia – presumably consisting of descendents of the ancient Vikings – hold rowing races on the river. Be warned that, at York's 'popular price' (free), the crowds are often large.

In summer the river takes on a calmer life style. Visitors can take out self-drive motorboats and explore the city's river frontage for themselves.

A variety of large pleasure boats, some offering food and musical entertainment, make regular one-hour trips downstream to the Archbishop's Palace at Bishopthorpe. There are plans for some excursions to go ashore and explore the home of the Archbishop of York, and the palace gardens have been opened to the public. Some boat companies also offer floodlit evening cruises stopping off for supper at a riverside public house. Pre-booked parties, by arrangement, can explore further downstream to Naburn and upstream to Nether Poppleton.

Ghost Walks

York was the first city in the country to set up ghost walks and with a proliferation of ghoulish local tales, it has been named the 'Most Haunted City in Europe'. A variety of companies lead tours of the old city, some with more humorous guides than others. The Ghost Hunt of York tour is highly rated (tel: 01904 608700, www.ghosthunt.co.uk) other companies include the Original Ghost Walk of York (tel: 01759 373090, www.theoriginalghostwalkofyork.co.uk).

71

The final furlong

Relaxing by the river

Getting There

Opposite: a tranquil evening on the Ouse

By car

York is about four hours from London, an hour and a half from Manchester, two hours from Newcastle upon Tyne and four hours from Edinburgh. The M1 motorway from London reaches Leeds 24 miles (40km) from York and continues as the A1 until the start of the A1 (M) to Newcastle. Bramham crossroads on the A1, some 12 miles (20km) west of York, is the city's main link with the motorway network. The approach to York from the A1 is by the A64 which is now all dual carriageway. The cross Pennine M62, which leads to Manchester, runs some 20 miles (32 km) south of the city and it can be reached either via the A1 or by a much slower route through Selby or Howden.

For local radio travel information, BBC Radio York is on 828 kHz MW, 95.5 MHz VHF; independent Minster FM is on 104.7 VHF.

Restricted access to cars

By coach

National Express runs a direct coach service between London and York four times every day, as well as regular services from other main towns in the UK. Though slower, it is much cheaper than travelling by train. The journey from London takes a minimum of four-and-a-half hours when you travel directly. The setting down point in York is in Rougier Street. To book, tel: 08705 808080.

73

By train

Fast Intercity trains link York with London and Scotland. There is a half-hourly service between York and London with the journey time between 1hr 50 minutes and 2hrs 20 minutes. Trains leave London from King's Cross station (tel: 08457 484950).

Trains from York to Scarborough, Filey and Bridlington on the coast run very regularly, and six trains an hour run to Leeds. A twice-hourly shuttle service operates between the city and Manchester Airport.

York Railway Station is only a few minutes from the centre of the city but you might want to take advantage of the taxi rank in the portico, or the Hertz car rental agency.

York Railway Station

By air

The nearest airports to York are Leeds/Bradford (north west of Leeds) some 25 miles (40km) from York, tel: 0113 2509696 and Robin Hood Airport in Sheffield, 35 miles (55km) from York tel: 0870 833 2210.

A train shuttle service runs to Manchester Airport. For information on flights to and from the airport, tel: 0161 489 3000.

Getting Around

York is a 'walkable' city and maps are available in the Tourist Information Centres (*see* Facts for the Visitor, *page 75*). Open-top bus tours also offer a hop on and hop off service. City Sightseeing Tours run all year, Guide Friday tours run only in summer. Tickets for either can be bought at the Tourist Office or from the driver and are valid for 24 hours from purchase. Tickets also allow some discounts to a handful of city sites. In high season buses run every 10 minutes between 9.30am and 5.30pm.

York is easy to explore

Car Rental

York is an ideal day-trip centre for exploring country and coast. Car rental firms include:

Hertz, York Station, tel: 01904 612586.
      US: 800-654-3131
      UK: 0870 850 2677
      www.hertz.co.uk
Polar Self Drive, tel: 01904 615008.

Buses

Excursions are run to nearby towns and villages (York Pullman Bus Company, tel: 01904 622992). Another popular service is the Moorsbus (tel: 01845 597000) that connects York with Whitby and other seaside towns via numerous towns and villages in the North York Moors National Park.

York has recently unveiled a sleek new public bus fleet that is managed with satellite tracking technology, which allows traffic lights to change for approaching buses and should help prevent lengthy traffic delays.

Taxis

Taxis can not be hailed on the street but there are taxi ranks outside the train station and the City Art Gallery (nights only). Otherwise you must ring for them to collect you.
Station Taxis, tel: 01904 623332.
Ace Taxis, tel: 01904 638888.
Fleetway Taxis: 01904 645333.

Car parks

You may want to park your car in York, but it is best to avoid doing so if you can. If you must park in the city in summer, it is best to use one of the five park-and-ride schemes: from Askham Bar on the A64 southern approach to the city; at Rawcliffe Bar on the western section of the city bypass; at Grimston Bar off the eastern section; at the Designer Outlet off the southern section close to the A19; and at Monks Cross on the Malton Road northeast of the city. Parking is free, though of course there is a charge for using the frequent bus service into the city centre.

If you really need to park closer there are car parks in Union Terrace outside Monk Bar, at Jewbury, St George's Field, Marygate and the Castle Car Park – if you can get in. There is multi-storey car parking at the Shambles Car Park in Garden Place and at the Piccadilly Car Park. Charges for all the central car parks are by the hour and a long stay can be very expensive, so much so that a phone line has been set up to accept payment via credit card. After all few people have enough pocket change for a day's parking in York. If you are staying in the city centre, it's best to leave your car parked at the hotel or guesthouse for the duration of your stay.

Transport in the city centre

Facts for the Visitor

Tourist Information

The city has two tourist information centres, both of which have a range of guidebooks, maps and information. They will also take bookings for accommodation, tours and excursions. You will find them at:
De Grey Rooms, Exhibition Square, tel: 01904 621756.
George Hudson Street, tel: 01904 554653.
In addition there is the National Trust Shop and Information Centre at 32 Goodramgate, tel: 01904 659050.

York Pass

Valid for up to three days, the York Pass gives free entry to popular attractions plus discounts for some restaurants, car hire and entertainments. You can buy it online at www.yorkpass.com or tel: 01904 550099. They are also for sale at the tourist information centres.

Hop on and off all day

Sightseeing tours

Open-top buses tour parts of the city that can still be reached on wheels, hop-on and hop-off, all day (*see page 74*).

Garden blooms

Walking guided tours start from Exhibition Square. Moreover, a number of ghost-walk organisers compete for passing customers *(see page 71)*. You will probably see their plaques and posters, complete with details and timings, around the city centre.

Opening times

York is 'open' all year round but visiting for most of the stately homes in the vicinity is seasonal, usually Easter to October. Many of York's city centre shops are open on Sundays, particularly during the summer.

Postal services

The main post office is situated at 22 Lendal (Monday to Friday 9am–5.30pm, Saturday 9am–12.30pm). The regional sorting office is in Leeman Road near the Marble Arch Railway Bridge and is useful for late-night posting of urgent mail.

Emergencies

Police, ambulance, fire brigade, tel: 999.
York Police Station, tel: 01904 631321.

Spectator Sports

York City Football Club, Kit Kat Crescent, tel: 0870 777 1922, www.ycfc.net.
York Rugby League Club, tel: 01904 421075.
York Rugby Union FC, Clifton Park, tel: 01904 623602.
York Cricket Club, Clifton Park, tel: 01904 623602, www.yorkcricketclub.com.
Races, Knavesmire, flat meetings May and October, tel: 01904 620911, www.yorkracecourse.co.uk.
Fulford Golf Club, Heslington Lane, (venue for golf tournaments): tel: 01904 413 579, www.fulfordgolfclub.co.uk.
Point to Points, Whitwell on the Hill, near Malton, in May.

Let loose at the Air Museum

Events

A number of events are staged every year, from charity markets to music festivals and medieval weekends. For details call the Event Hotline: 01904 554430.

York for Children

York is 'child friendly' and the best parts for children are free. Central areas are all safely pedestrianised and the ramparts of the **Bar Walls** have sturdy railings so young-sters can not only enjoy the view but 'shoot' invaders through real arrow slits. On summer days the Museum Gardens provide an ideal family picnic spot and a place for letting off steam. Buskers and street performers keep young and old continually entertained in King's Square and Parliament Street.

The city's museums have adapted to family needs. The **National Railway Museum** is a small child's paradise. Not far from the city's real railway station is the **York Model Railway Centre** where young visitors can set trains running through miniature cities and countryside. But many of the principal sites have areas providing special events for children, too. Inside the **Minster** *(see page 16)* fact sheets and 'trails' can be acquired and the **City Art Gallery** *(see page 22)* has treasure hunts among the Old Masters. The new **Jorvik Viking Centre** *(see page 31)* enthralls youngsters with its time car ride through Viking York and the **Castle Museum** *(see page 33)* chills and delights young visitors with its condemned cell and cobbled streets. The **Yorkshire Museum** *(see page 42)*, which has permanent period galleries and visiting exhibitions, always features some 'hands on' experience for young visitors.

Jorvik Viking Centre

Archaeology made interesting at DIG

DIG (the Archaeological Resource Centre) in St Saviourgate is all 'hands on' with young visitors encouraged to hunt through trays of 'dig debris' and extract pottery, bones and other 'finds.' They can also 'explore' ancient buildings with the aid of hi-tech computer screens.

There are a number of places of interest for children outside the city, making good days out. Further afield children will enjoy **Beningbrough Hall** *(see page 57)* which has an adventure playground in the shrubbery and a huge walled garden set aside for picnics. Stately **Castle Howard** *(see page 57)* has a playground down by the lake with a road 'train' running around the estate to ease the walking.

Down on the farm

Pickering, 25 miles (40 km) north of the city, has a double attraction – a **steam train service** which runs across the North York Moors to Goathland, and one of the most outstanding castles in the county. The **Yorkshire Air Museum** *(see page 59)* is another day out. And of course the seaside is not far away.

Royal York

Accommodation

In summer, particularly during race meetings and festivals, it is safer to book accommodation ahead. Tourist Information Centres will help to find somewhere to stay. B&Bs can be found in a wide area around the city.

Hotels
£££ (Over £120 per night double)

Dean Court, Duncombe Place, tel: 01904 625082, www.deancourt-york.co.uk. Comfortable, traditional hotel close to the Minster and in its own traffic-free zone.

The Grange, Clifton, tel: 01904 644744, www.grange-hotel.co.uk. Regency town house with a restful air and open fires in cold weather.

Middlethorpe Hall

Hilton Hotel, Tower Street, www.hilton.co.uk, tel: 01904 648111. A large, modern hotel overlooking Clifford's Tower and close to the heart of the city.

Middlethorpe Hall, near Bishopthorpe, tel: 01904 641241, www.middlethorpe.com. An elegant country hotel set in a 17th-century house and run with style and grace. On the outskirts of York and not far from the racecourse.

Park Inn York, North Street, www.rezidorparkinn.com, tel; 01904 459988. A smart multi-storey hotel, on the south bank of the river. Ideally situated in the city centre, facilities include sauna, solarium and gymnasium.

Royal York, Station Road, tel: 01904 653681. A Victorian railway hotel in the grand style, with imposing public rooms, impressive dining room and fine views across the gardens to the cathedral.

York Marriott, Tadcaster Road, tel: 01904 701000, www.yorkmarriott.co.uk. Overlooking the famous racecourse and with extensive leisure facilities plus a courtesy bus into town.

££ (Over £70 per night double)

Abbots Mews, Marygate, tel: 01904 634866. Originally a coachman's cottage, the building was converted in 1976 into an attractive two-storey hotel. Near Museum Gardens.
Churchill Hotel, Bootham, www.churchillhotel.com, tel: 01904 644456. Converted Georgian residence in its own grounds near city centre. Ample parking.
Holiday Inn, Tadcaster Road, tel: 0870 4009085. On the road into town, overlooking the racecourse.
Jarvis Abbey Park, The Mount, tel: 01904 658301. A former Georgian town house converted into a comfortable 85-bedroom hotel five minutes' walk from the city walls.
Judges Lodging, www.judgeslodgings.com, tel: 01904 638733. Grand Georgian town house, centrally placed.
Kilima, Holgate Road, www.kilima.co.uk, tel: 01904 625787. Spacious, friendly hotel in former Victorian rectory.
Lady Anne Middleton's Hotel, www.ladyannes.co.uk, tel: 01904 611570. Well-situated near city centre and the river.
Mount Royale, The Mount, www.mountroyale.co.uk, tel: 01904 628856. Comfortable, secluded and with good leisure facilities.
Novotel, Fishergate, tel: 01904 611660. Family hotel with swimming pool and children's playground.
Savages, St Peter's Grove, tel: 01904 610818. Victorian town house which has been turned into a comfortable family hotel within easy walking distance of the city centre.
York Pavilion Hotel, Main Street, Fulford, tel: 01904 622099, www.yorkpavilionhotel.com. Relaxed atmosphere, award-winning cuisine.

Jarvis Abbey Park

79

£ (Under £70 per night double)

Bootham Bar Hotel, High Petergate, tel: 01904 65816, www.fourhighpetergate.co.uk. Well-situated beside one of the city's ancient gateways within yards of the Minster.
Curzon Lodge, Tadcaster Road, tel: 01904 703157. Former 17th-century farmhouse with cottage-style bedrooms, beams and antiques. Overlooking the racecourse.
Galtres Lodge, Low Petergate, tel: 01904 622478. Family-run hotel in Georgian town house in the heart of the city.
Jorvik Hotel, Marygate, www.jorvikhotel.co.uk, tel: 01904 653511. En suite accommodation a few minutes from the Minster.
Knavesmire Manor Hotel, Tadcaster Road, tel: 01904 702941, www.knavesmire.co.uk. Georgian house overlooking the racecourse and noted for its cuisine.
Riverside Walk Guest House, Earlsborough Terrace, tel: 01904 620769, www.riversidewalkyork.com. On the river's edge, close to the city centre and the railway station.
York International Youth Hostel, Clifton, tel: 01904 653147, www.yha.org.uk. Award-winning centre with gardens and catering.

Index